How to Live a Holy Life

Devotions for Living in This Century

Jim Young

Warner House Press

REVIEWS OF THE PREVIOUS EDITION

Pastor Jim and I have had many conversations and prayers together over the years. I've known Jim as a great pastor, leader, and friend. Now I can also say, "I know him as a great writer!" You will truly be blessed by the words and writings of Jim, as he interweaves all his experiences of ministry, military, and life into his work to encourage you to keep the faith. It's very evident that Pastor Jim has poured his heart into his writings, so as you read, allow your heart to be inspired to to also live a faith-filled life as the writer does himself!

Pastor Cid Cota

How to live a holy life is a powerful and life-changing read as author and pastor, Jim Young, brings the scriptures to life each day in a relevant and applicable way. I am so grateful for Jim's humble and wise voice in my life through his devotions!

Pastor Travis Clark

Pastor Young was our pastor for 4 years. He is a godly man, firmly planted in God's word. I was excited to read Pastor Young's devotional. It is full of truth to keep us focused on living our life to bring glory to God. I will read and re-read this book many times. Thank you Pastor Young for this awesome legacy.

Dale (Skip) Albin

A Labor of Love. We have been blessed by Pastor Young's book of devotions. Every page provides lessons for life. If we have worries or questions about everyday concerns, the devotions give us comfort and guidance that help us understand and cope with those issues. Every devotion has it's root in God's Holy Word and Pastor Young has written each of them with Love through Faith. We hope you will find them as much of a blessing as we have.

Larry and Vicki Cox Blanchard, Oklahoma

This is a greatly expanded version of an edition privately distributed in 2022.

Published by Warner House Press of Albertville, Alabama USA 2024
Copyright © 2024 Jim Young
Cover Artwork © Lisa Holliday Heilman 2024
Print Design © 2024 Warner House Press

Warner House Press
1325 Lane Switch Road
Albertville, Alabama 35951
USA

ISBN: 978-1-951890-47-6 (Pbk) 978-1-951890-54-4 (ePub)

CONTENTS

This book is dedicated to my dad, Mack Young.

He was a Godly, hard-working man who taught me how to live a Godly life.

He taught an adult Sunday school class for over 20 years

and he knew the Bible from front to back.

He was very kind and patient, he never turned down anyone who needed help.

"For I know the plans I have for you," declares the Lord, "plans to prosper you and not to harm you, plans to give you hope and a future. Then you will call on me and come and pray to me, and I will listen to you. You will seek me and find me when you seek me with all your heart."

Jeremiah 29:11–13 NIV

A CALL TO WORSHIP AND OBEDIENCE

> *Oh come, let us sing to the Lord!*
> *Let us shout joyfully to the Rock of our salvation.*
> *Let us come before His presence with thanksgiving;*
> *Let us shout joyfully to Him with psalms.*
> *For the Lord is the great God, And the great King above all gods.*
>
> Psalm 95:1–4 NKJV

There is coming a day very soon when we shall all bow down to the One and only God: Our Lord and Savior Jesus Christ. We shall shout our praises to the one true God for there shall be no other.

The Lord demands true worship and obedience above all things. The biggest problem most people have with being committed to Lord is that they still want to do things their own way. Americans especially are very independent people and the idea of surrendering their will and how they live their lives is a very difficult thing to do. This country was founded on the right to be independent, especially when it involves freedom of religion. There are many religions in the world, but there is only one true God. There is a big difference between being committed to a religion and being devoted to the one true God, Jesus Christ. There is freedom in being a child of Christ that no other religion can offer. Freedom from sin, addictions, and bondage that only Christ can offer. That is a great reason to give praise and obedience to the one true God.

A LITTLE GOOD NEWS

There is a lot of uncertainty in the world today and people are searching everywhere for good news, not the continuous bad news on TV. People are scared about the things they are seeing and hearing. People are never going to find good news on the pages of a newspaper, the evening news, or on Facebook. Our only hope for good news is by realizing what Jesus Christ did on the cross over 2000 years ago. The message of the cross is the good news!

> *Peace I leave with you, My peace I give to you; not as the world gives do I give to you. Let not your heart be troubled, neither let it be afraid. You have heard me say to you, "I am going away and coming back to you." If you loved Me, you would rejoice because I said, "I am going to the Father," for My Father is greater than I.*
>
> John 14:27–28 NKJV

We don't know when Jesus is coming back, but until then He will give us the Holy Spirit to comfort us. All we have to do is trust Him and He is more than capable of taking care of us until He returns.

A NEW DAY COMING

> *For behold, I create a new heaven and a new earth;*
> *And the former shall not be remembered or come to mind.*
>
> Isaiah 65:17 NKJV

As we see all of the things that are happening in the world today, and it seems as if everything is spinning out of control, don't be discouraged! The Bible promises us there is a new heaven and a new earth coming. All the things of this world will no longer be remembered. Our sins will be forgiven and forgotten. Satan will be thrown into the lake of fire and there will be rejoicing forever, as we worship our Lord and Savior Jesus Christ throughout eternity. One of the most common questions people have is: "Will the things I have done in the past be remembered?" Or, they say it is too late for them because of all the things they have done. Isaiah 65:17 answers both of those questions. When God forgives you of your sins, the past is no longer remembered, and it truly is a new day. It is never too late to ask forgiveness for your sins and begin a new chapter in your life, and eventually you will be with Christ in a new heaven and new earth. Oh, what a day that will be!

ALL SCRIPTURE IS GOD-BREATHED

> All Scripture is God-breathed and is useful for teaching, rebuking, correcting and training in righteousness, so that the man of God may be thoroughly equipped for every good work. In the presence of God and of Christ Jesus, who will judge the living and the dead, and in view of his appearing and his kingdom, I give you this charge: Preach the Word; be prepared in season and out of season; correct, rebuke and encourage—with great patience and careful instruction. For the time will come when men will not put up with sound doctrine. Instead, to suit their own desires, they will gather around them a great number of teachers to say what their itching ears want to hear. They will turn their ears away from the truth and turn aside to myths. But you, keep your head in all situations, endure hardship, do the work of an evangelist, discharge all the duties of your ministry.
>
> 2 Timothy 3:16–4:5 NIV84

Paul said all scripture is God breathed and useful for teaching, rebuking, correcting, and training. I believe in the inerrancy of the scriptures; that means I believe the whole Bible is true and we are to read and teach the whole Bible, not just the parts we like or agree with. Paul is encouraging Timothy to have the courage to speak the truth and not to be intimidated by those who don't like what he has to say. Many churches today have watered down the gospel and won't talk about the more controversial subjects for fear of offending people. We are living in an age of extreme tolerance, where we are told to be respectful of other people's beliefs and opinions. I respect other people's right to have their own beliefs and opinions; God gives everybody the option of believing what the Bible teaches is true. The Bible wasn't written to please people; it wasn't written as a book of suggestions on how we are to live. It was written as the word of God to teach us how to live a holy life that is pleasing to Him. The Bible isn't about you and what you think. It is about obedience to a Holy God. God hasn't changed; what He said was sin and an abomination to Him. A stench in His nostrils thousands of years ago still is today. Just because society has changed its attitudes about what is morally and socially acceptable doesn't mean God has changed His mind about things. Now, some people would call that narrow minded; I call it having the mind of God. God said He is the same yesterday, today, and forever.

So how do you gain that desire to read and study the Bible? First, pray about it. Ask God to give you wisdom and understanding as you read to make the things you are reading come alive so that you may apply it to your life. Next, if you have never read through the Bible before don't start with the Old Testament. It can be very difficult to understand because it talks a lot about the history of mankind and a lot of the Levitical laws the Jews were required to follow under the law. The book of John is the best place to start reading the Bible because John gives a very good account of why Jesus came to earth in the first place and why we should believe He is the savior. When you read the Bible, don't just read it like any other book; it is meant to be meditated on and studied. When you just quickly read over scripture without thinking about what it is saying, you are missing the whole point of reading the Bible. You don't read the Bible for entertainment, you read it to learn and to have it speak to you. There are some things in the Bible that were culturally specific to that period of time, but there are things within those things that are timeless truths. The animal sacrifices in the Old Testament, for example, were about obedience to God and bringing your best before him. We are still to bring our best or ourselves before him today.

Today, what we bring before Him may not be animals, but it could be money, time, talents or many other things, as long as it is the very best we have to honor our Savior.

ALL YOU NEED TODAY IS JESUS

> *O Lord, if you heal me, I will be truly healed;*
> *if you save me, I will be truly saved.*
> *My praises are for you alone!*
>
> Jeremiah 17:14 NLT

If only people would realize how true this prayer by the prophet Jeremiah is. People will try all kinds of things to get through the day. Some people think they can't get through the day without coffee and cigarettes. Others have to read their daily horoscope for their strength. Jesus knows you better than you know yourself, he knows what you need, and when you need it. He is your healer, your savior and your everlasting King of kings.

The only thing you need today is Jesus! He is your healer and your redeemer. Give him praise in all things and in every situation, for there is nothing or nobody greater than Him. He is I AM, the everlasting God, and the great physician. Give your troubles to Him today and rest in his promises, to be there always.

ARE YOU TOO SMART FOR YOUR OWN GOOD?

> *Then the chief priests and the Pharisees gathered a council and said, "What shall we do? For this Man works many signs. If we let Him alone like this, everyone will believe in Him, and the Romans will come and take away both our place and nation." And one of them, Caiaphas, being high priest that year, said to them, "You know nothing at all, nor do you consider that it is expedient for us that one man should die for the people, and not that the whole nation should perish." Now this he did not say on his own authority; but being high priest that year he prophesied that Jesus would die for the nation, and not for that nation only, but also that He would gather together in one the children of God who were scattered abroad. Then, from that day on, they plotted to put Him to death.*
>
> John 11:47–53 NKJV

Caiaphas was the high priest of a religious group known as the Sadducees. They were well educated, wealthy, and politically influential. The Sadducees hated Jesus because he threatened their influential life style. They could not accept his message: The servants would become leaders and the leaders would become servants. Caiaphas inherited his position because he was the male heir from the descendants of Aaron, and it was a lifetime position. He thought his position was secure, and wasn't about to let anyone spoil it. It was his policy to remove any threats to his power by whatever means necessary—even murder.

There are a lot of people today who have the same mindset of Caiaphas—even Christians. They will do anything for power. They will do anything to keep their lifestyle from being threatened. They think they know all the answers and have everything figured out to their advantage. Elections are evidence of how far people will go obtain power. They think nothing of trying to ruin someone else's reputation. The ENRON scandal is a perfect example of powerful people cheating common folks out of their life savings in order to make millions for themselves.

There are some things Caiaphas didn't consider, and neither do some people today:

- We should never do something evil so that something good will happen.

- It is really easy to justify doing something by saying, "Who's going to know?"

- Thinking "So what if somebody gets hurt? This is for the greater good."

- Doing harm to someone else—physically, emotionally or financially—is never the answer.

It was not certain that Christ would be acknowledged as king by all the people, or that he would lead a revolt against the Romans. Jumping to conclusions is one of the worst things we can do. A person should always carefully check his facts and study the situation carefully before drawing a hasty conclusion. If Caiaphas had learned more about Jesus and his purpose for being here on earth, he would have realized that Jesus had no intention of being an earthly king, or interfering with the Roman government. Jesus was talking about a heavenly kingdom, but Caiaphas was so self absorbed and concerned about himself that he couldn't see that or even understand what Jesus was talking about.

Don't underestimate the wisdom and counsel of others around you. Caiaphas accused other people of being stupid because, in their opinion, Jesus was not a threat.

"You know nothing at all, nor do you consider that it is expedient for us that one man should die for the people, and not that the whole nation should perish."

John 11:49–50

Caiaphas meant it would be better for Jesus to die rather than the Jews have trouble with the Romans. It was true that Jesus should die to save the nation, but not in the way that Caiaphas meant. It was true in a far greater and more wonderful way than Caiaphas could have ever imagined.

For the message of the cross is foolishness to those who are perishing, but to us who are being saved it is the power of God. For it is written: "I will destroy the wisdom of the wise, and bring to nothing the understanding of the prudent." Where is the wise? Where is the scribe? Where is the disputer of this age? Has not God made foolish the wisdom of this world?

1 Corinthians 1:18–20 NKJV

Do you see a man wise in his own eyes? There is more hope for a fool than for him.

Proverbs 26:12 NKJV

In the end, the attempts at wisdom that Caiaphas made, his scheming and plotting, were all useless. About eight or nine years after Jesus was brought before him, a new Roman governor came to Jerusalem and Caiaphas was deposed.

Here are some additional thoughts to consider:

- In the past, God used bad people and bad situations for His glory:

  ◦ Jacob and Esau;

- Joseph;

- And, especially, the death of Jesus Christ.

- Even today, God can take bad people and bad situations and use them for his glory:

  - 9-11;

  - Hurricane Katrina;

  - Charles Colson's role in Watergate and subsequent imprisonment;

  - Nicky Cruz and his gang membership before conversion (read *Run, Baby, Run*).

- God has a huge advantage over the rest of us:

  - He knows what the results of our actions are going to be;

  - He knows what is going to happen in the future;

  - He can take our lemons and make them into lemonade.

Wouldn't it be wonderful if everybody looked to God for advice before making a decision? We could save ourselves so much heartache and trouble.

Make up your mind today that you are going to trust God with the decisions you make, no matter how important or seemingly insignificant. Nothing going on in our lives is too small for God to help us with, but we have to be willing to let him. God doesn't go where he is not wanted. So the next time you make a decision, go to God first and make it a matter of prayer. You will be glad you did.

ATHEIST LEADERSHIP IN THE CHURCH

> *If anyone wants to provide leadership in the church, good! But there are preconditions: A leader must be well-thought-of, committed to his wife, cool and collected, accessible, and hospitable. He must know what he's talking about, not be overfond of wine, not pushy but gentle, not thin-skinned, not money-hungry. He must handle his own affairs well, attentive to his own children and having their respect. For if someone is unable to handle his own affairs, how can he take care of God's church? He must not be a new believer, lest the position go to his head and the Devil trip him up. Outsiders must think well of him, or else the Devil will figure out a way to lure him into his trap.*
>
> 1 Timothy 3:1–7 MSG

I read an article yesterday about Harvard University appointing an atheist as a humanist chaplain to meet the needs of those who don't have any religious beliefs.

atheist | ˈāTHēəst | Noun A person who disbelieves or lacks belief in the existence of God or gods. *"he is a committed atheist"* chaplain | 'CHaplən Noun a member of the clergy attached to a private chapel, institution, ship, branch of the armed forces, etc. *"a prison chaplain"*

A chaplain—by definition—is someone who helps people in various situations deal with their spirituality and draw closer to God. I was a hospice chaplain and a hospital chaplain for about eight years, and very much enjoyed helping people find a closer relationship with God during a very difficult time in their lives. To me the term *atheist chaplain* is an oxymoron. For Harvard University, a college that was founded on biblical principles and beliefs, to welcome someone who would undermine the very calling of a chaplain to minister to people, and to open the door for Satan to pervert Christianity even further in a very liberal secular school, is one more step down the road to communism in the United States of America. We used to be one nation under God. What happened?[1]

---

1. Brown, Michael, *When Harvard hired an atheist to be the chief university chaplain*, The Christian Post, August 31, 2021; accessed October 27th, 2022 via https://www.christianpost.com/voices/when-harvard-hired-an-atheist-to-be-the-chief-university-chaplain.html

BALANCE IS THE KEY

One of Satan's biggest tools is to keep us unbalanced. In order to do that, he appeals to all of our emotions. We are subject to his influence through the body, the soul, and the spirit.

> *For our struggle is not against flesh and blood, but against the rulers, against the authorities, against the powers of this dark world and against the spiritual forces of evil in the heavenly realms.*
>
> Ephesians 6:12 NIV

Satan is able to get to us through our own pride and selfishness. That is how He got to Eve in the Garden of Eden: First he appealed to her flesh by telling her the fruit was good to eat. Then he appealed to her senses by showing her how good it looked. Then he appealed to her pride by telling her it would make her wise and she would be very knowledgeable. We all have these same emotions, and we all respond to them in different ways. God responds to us through these same emotions but in a different way. God wants us to have balance in our lives and put our trust in Him when we have problems. Satan wants us to be unbalanced and upset all the time. He wants our lives to be full of confusion and chaos. When our lives are chaotic, we don't have time to think about the things of God. The beauty of the gospel is that it appeals to all of our senses and shows us how to live a balanced life in the way God would have us to. Sometimes people want treatment for the symptoms and not the disease. God doesn't work that way. He offers a solution to your problem, and he doesn't just treat the symptoms. It would be like a person with cancer telling a doctor to ignore the cancer and just treat the rash he has on his arm. No good doctor is going to ignore the cancer and just treat the rash. The doctor is going to want to solve all of that person's symptoms—not just the one. Jesus always goes to the heart of the problem.

BE CAREFUL WHAT YOU ASK FOR

When Tom Landry was coaching the Dallas Cowboys, he was quoted as saying:

"I have a job to do that is not very complicated, but it is often difficult to get a group of men to do what they don't want to do so they can achieve the one thing they have wanted all their lives."

Coach Landry, in that seemingly contradictory statement, described what discipline is all about: doing what we don't want to do so we can accomplish what we have always wanted.

Grace and salvation are not complicated, but it is often very difficult to get people to spend time in prayer and bible study in order get what they have always wanted, and that is experiencing the joy and the glory that is achieved by being in the presence of God.

Grace is free, but it isn't cheap. It requires us doing our best every day to model our lives after Jesus Christ. Jesus Christ gave his life so we could experience the grace of God. I would say that was a pretty steep price to pay.

We have to be open to whatever it is God is trying to do in our lives, and it isn't always what we ask for—or even expect. Doing anything in this life that is worth effort is not easy. It almost always requires a lot of hard work and putting in the

time and effort it requires. Serving Jesus Christ is a 24 hour a day, 7 day a week commitment. All the promises made in the Bible are true, but we have to do our part receive those things.

This poem by an anonymous author says it all:

I asked God for strength that I might achieve;
I was made weak that I might learn to humbly obey.
I asked for health, that I might do greater things;
I was given infirmity, that I might do better things.
I asked for riches, that I might be happy;
I was given poverty, that I might be wise,
I asked for power, that I might have the praise of men;
I was given weakness, that I might feel the need of God.
I asked for all things, that I might enjoy life;
I was given life, that I might enjoy all things.
I got nothing that I asked for, but everything I had hoped for.
I am, among all men, most richly blessed.

BE KIND TO EVERYONE

> *Be wise in the way you act toward outsiders; make the most of every opportunity. Let your conversation be always full of grace, seasoned with salt, so that you may know how to answer everyone.*
>
> Colossians 4:5–6 NIV

Sometimes saying and doing the right thing can be very difficult. Our mouth tends to get us in more trouble than any other part of our bodies. It is very important to think before we respond to people, especially in the heat of the moment, when we are more likely to say something, we can't take back. It always helps to take a deep breath and think about what we want to say. I am guilty of saying things I wish I could take back and that is something I have to live with. There is an old saying, "You can catch more flies with honey." You can make and keep friends by thinking before you speak and saying a quick prayer before you say anything.

> *All kinds of animals, birds, reptiles and sea creatures are being tamed and have been tamed by mankind, but no human being can tame the tongue. It is a restless evil, full of deadly poison. With the tongue we praise our Lord*

and Father, and with it we curse human beings, who have been made in God's likeness.

James 3:7–9 NIV

BE STILL AND KNOW THAT I AM GOD

> Come and see what the Lord has done,
> the desolations he has brought on the earth.
> He makes wars cease
> to the ends of the earth.
> He breaks the bow and shatters the spear;
> He burns the shields with fire.
> He says, "Be still, and know that I am God;
> I will be exalted among the nations,
> I will be exalted in the earth."
> The Lord Almighty is with us;
> the God of Jacob is our fortress.
>
> Psalm 46:8–11 NIV

Have you ever thought that perhaps God is talking to you, but you are not listening? You need to find a quiet place where there are no distractions and just listen for the voice of the Holy Spirit. There is so much noise around us no matter where we are; it can be at work, at home, or just about anywhere we go.

I have found the best place for me is in my car, with windows up and the radio off.

I am not saying take your eyes off the road; just be quiet and drive. Listening is very hard for some people. They are concentrating so hard on what they want to say and not listening to what other people are saying. Just sitting quietly and listening can be a very soothing and refreshing experience.

Just clear your mind of everything and listen for that still, small voice.

Sometimes, just laying in bed at night, I listen for that voice. Maybe you are going through a rough time right now and have been praying for God to help you. Maybe you didn't hear the answer because you were not listening. Find that quiet place wherever it may be and "Be still and know that I am God." Be patient and listen for that still, small voice and you will hear the answer. It may not be the answer you want, but it will be the right answer, because God is leading you in the right direction.

BE STRONG AND COURAGEOUS

> *So be strong and courageous! Do not be afraid and do not panic before them.*
> *For the Lord your God will personally go ahead of you.*
> *He will neither fail you nor Abandon you.*
>
> Deuteronomy 3:16 NLT

What a comforting thought: To know that God is going to be with us no matter what we are facing. If you are going through something right now that is making you fearful, know that the God of the Universe is with you and he will see you through it. He is not going to abandon you in the middle of the ocean and make you swim to shore. If the ship sinks, he will carry you on his shoulders. Whatever it is just give it to God and you will get through this; that is a promise straight from God himself.

It is very hard to give control of a very difficult and even life-threatening situation to someone else, even God himself. It takes a lot of strength and courage to be able to say, "I leave this in your hands, Lord, and I trust you to help me get through this, because I know I don't have the strength within myself to make it through."

A lot of times it takes being in a position where God is the only one who can help for someone give up control and let God be in charge. Sometimes people think they are being strong and courageous by trying to fight a battle themselves and are determined to beat whatever it is by themselves. In reality, it takes more strength and courage to turn it over to God and give him complete control. That was the situation with the Children of Israel; they were very stubborn and not willing to listen to Moses who was getting his instructions from God. Eventually their stubbornness cost them seeing the Promised Land because of their rebelliousness.

Their children and grandchildren saw the Promised Land because they listened to Joshua and the instructions God gave him.

BEFORE

> *For You formed my inward parts;*
> *You covered me in my mother's womb.*
> *I will praise You, for I am fearfully and wonderfully made;*
> *Marvelous are Your works,*
> *And that my soul knows very well.*
> *My frame was not hidden from You,*
> *When I was made in secret,*
> *And skillfully wrought in the lowest parts of the earth.*
> *Your eyes saw my substance, being yet unformed.*
> *And in Your book they all were written,*
> *The days fashioned for me,*
> *When as yet there were none of them.*
>
> Psalm 139:13–16 NKJV

Before you can love yourself, you have to let God love you. Before you can love others, you have to love yourself. Before you can help others, you have to be able to help yourself. Before God can use you, you need to know his plan for your life and follow it. Before you can do anything you must pray and ask God what to do. God loved you before you were even born. He loves you now and wants only the best for you.

It is beyond my comprehension to think that before the world was even formed, He knew you.

He knew when you were born, and He knows when you are going to die.

Yet, He asks nothing in return; He loves you and wants the best for you. He is not going force you to do anything. He gave you free will to make the choices in life you want to make, but yet He is patiently waiting for you to come to him and follow the path that He already has laid out for you.

If you feel lost and confused trying to figure out what to do next, try praying and asking God to show you His plan for your life. Even if you have made a lot of mistakes, He will put you back on the right path. All you have to do is ask Him and He will help you find the way that you should go in order to have peace and contentment with God and yourself.

Search me, O God, and know my heart;
Try me, and know my anxieties;
And see if there is any wicked way in me,
And lead me in the way everlasting.

Psalm 139:23–24 NKJV

BEING CONTENT

> *I know what it is to be in need, and I know what it is to have plenty. I have learned the secret of being content in any and every situation, whether well fed or hungry, whether living in plenty or in want. I can do everything through him who gives me strength.*
>
> Philippians 4:12–13 NIV84

Paul had learned the secret of contentment, and it wasn't anything the world had provided him. He was grateful for the things that people had sent him, but even without those things, he knew his strength and his rest came from the Lord. Paul was a man who had known wealth and privilege, and he realized those things did not bring him happiness, because those things are only temporary. Our outward circumstances are constantly changing and we cannot depend on those things. People gain and lose fortunes every day; people lose their homes through earthquakes, fires, and hurricanes. People lose loved ones through sickness and death, but the one constant we have in our lives is God. I like to say there is no such thing as a grumpy Christian. People are constantly complaining about one thing or another; it can be anything from their health to their bank account, to just about anything—just because they like to complain. Paul simply says that he knows how to be content and happy no matter what the circumstances. The world thinks that contentment means a good job, a nice house, and money in the bank. Paul is saying we don't need any of these things to be happy. All we need is the knowledge that Christ will supply all of our needs according to his riches in glory. Everything we have here is temporary and will all be gone someday. Our hope in Christ is all we have that will transfer to the next world when we die. In ancient times, kings who had those huge pyramids built did that because they had all of their wealth and worldly possessions sealed in the pyramid with them. I have heard of people today being buried in their favorite automobile. What a waste of a beautiful vehicle! If they knew Christ when they died, they will go to heaven, but all that other stuff will be left behind.

I have never seen a U-Haul behind a hearse.

BEING MARY

> But Mary treasured up all these things and pondered them in her heart. The shepherds returned, glorifying and praising God for all the things they have heard and seen, which were just as they had been told.
>
> Luke 2:19–20 NIV

Can you imagine being nine months pregnant and having to walk eighty miles, just to give birth in a dirty stable with cows witnessing your delivery? That is exactly what happened to Mary—it was eighty miles from Nazareth to Bethlehem. It would have been so much easier for her to have Jesus at home, but they were required to go to Bethlehem to be counted in the census being taken at the time. I would imagine that it probably took at least a week for them to get there, given Mary's condition. When they finally got there, they found all of the inns full and the only place they could find shelter was in the barn with the animals. It really wasn't even a barn; it was more like a lean-to, something to keep the wind and rain off the animals. It was fitting for Jesus to be born in such a humble situation because he came to save those who would humble themselves before him and accept his message of salvation. Jesus' ministry was to those who were down trodden and the poor of society. Joseph and Mary were both very humble people who lived very simple lives. They weren't royalty living in a palace; they lived in a small village called Nazareth where Joseph worked a carpenter and probably made barely enough to just get by.

Can you imagine using a feeding trough for animals as a crib? They put some hay in it and laid Jesus there because it was all they had. People today would be horrified at the unsanitary conditions he was born in. The swaddling clothes he was wrapped in were nothing more than strips of cloth that they wound around him, covering him from head to toe. Jesus' parents used what they had and made do with it.

Jesus lived and died as he was born, in very humble surroundings. He lived in small town and helped his father in his carpenter shop. When he began his ministry, he walked from town to town spreading His message. He didn't live in a fancy mansion or ride in a carriage; he was a very simple man who lived the message he spread. Everything he did was for the Glory of God.

Mary was probably very puzzled by how Jesus' life played out. She had given birth to the Son of God, yet he lived as a very poor humble man and had a very simple message. It wasn't until after his crucifixion and resurrection that she began to understand why he was born and died.

Girls in those days were not allowed to go to school. Their purpose in life was to marry, have babies, and maintain the household. So, it is no wonder Mary pondered everything in her heart, and I am sure she did that often throughout her life, and Jesus' life here on earth.

If a young maiden (probably 12 to 14) said *yes* to whatever the Lord wanted her to do, we should be able to do the same thing today, with all of the resources we have that Mary never had. She was a large part of the greatest event in history and didn't even realize it at the time.

BEING THERE FOR OTHERS

> *Keep on loving one another as brothers and sisters. Do not forget to show hospitality to strangers, for by so doing some people have shown hospitality to angels without knowing it.*
>
> Hebrews 13:1–2 NIV

You never know when you are going to have the opportunity to show Christ's love to someone. We need to be aware of what is going on around us, and be sensitive to the prompting of the Holy Spirit when he tells us to help someone who could use some assistance in their life. It could be something as simple as a prayer or an encouraging word or something more serious. Whatever it is, we should always be ready to serve those around us, doing what we can. The words of an old hymn say it best:

> *Others, Lord, yes, others,*
> *Let this my motto be;*
> *Help me to live for others,*
> *That I may live like Thee.*

Charles D. Meigs

If I see someone standing by the side of the road with sign saying they need help, I don't usually stop unless I feel the prompting of the Holy Spirit telling me to do it. There are a lot of people out there who do not need to be begging for money—that is why I always listen to the Holy Spirit. One time I saw someone standing by the road and I felt the Holy Spirit prompting me to stop, but I kept on going. The Holy Spirit doesn't give up that easy, so I finally stopped and turned around about half a mile down the road.

> *Give, and it will be given to you: good measure, pressed down, shaken together, and running over will be put into your bosom. For with the same measure that you use, it will be measured back to you.*
>
> Luke 6:38 NKJV

You can't out give the Lord; I have found that no matter what I have given, whether it be large or small, the Lord has always rewarded me in some way for helping that person, and there is no better feeling than helping someone in need.

BEST LAID PLANS

> *Many are the plans in a person's heart,*
> *but it is the Lord's purpose that prevails.*
>
> Proverbs 19:21 NIV

Planning and dreaming about the future is something that is a part of life and starts at an early age usually. They can be inspired by a TV show or a movie, even by something someone says. The best plans are the ones that God puts in our heart, but it is up to us to follow through on those plans. There are so many things today that can get our attention and distract us from those things. I remember growing up and having a lot of different plans that were constantly changing. Unfortunately, I didn't listen to the plans God had for me until much later in life. God has a way of reminding us of those plans and, even though we may go in a different direction, He will steer us in such a way that we don't even realize he is guiding us. I can look back on my life now and I can see those times when God guided me in such a way that that his plans eventually prevailed. It is never too late to let God take control of our lives and his plans for us can still be fulfilled. If you listen to the Holy Spirit and let God lead the way, you will realize that you are where God always wanted you to be. If you are searching for meaning and purpose in your life, try asking God to direct you. You won't regret it.

BLESSED IS THE MAN WHO TRUSTS IN THE LORD

> But blessed is the man who trusts in the Lord, whose confidence is in him. He will be like a tree planted by the water that sends out its roots by the stream. It does not fear when heat comes; its leaves are always green. It has no worries in a year of drought and never fails to bear fruit.
>
> Jeremiah 17:7–8 NIV

Trust Him.

A huge crowd was watching the famous tightrope walker, Charles Blondin, cross Niagara Falls one day in 1860. He crossed it numerous times—a 1,000 foot trip 160 feet above the raging waters. He not only walked across, he also pushed a wheelbarrow across. One little boy just stared in amazement. So, after completing a crossing, the fellow looked at the little boy and said, "Do you believe I could take a person across in the wheelbarrow without falling?"

"Yes, sir, I really do," the fellow says.

"Well then, get in, son."[1]

Are your roots deep enough to let God push the wheel barrow with you in it? Too many times when we face times of trouble, we wind up twisting in the wind and barely hanging on, because we are walking a spiritual tightrope and not trusting God to get us safely to the other side.

ISAIAH SAID THAT IF OUR ROOTS ARE DEEP ENOUGH, WE WILL NEVER FAIL TO BEAR FRUIT, EVEN IN THE HARD TIMES.

When we are going through hard times, people are watching us to see how we are going to react. Are we going to take the advice of Job's wife to curse God and die? Or are we going to stand strong knowing that our Redeemer lives and that nothing is going to take us out of his hands. Job stayed faithful to the Lord and he was rewarded with more than he had before.

Ah, Lord God! Behold, You have made the heavens and the earth by Your great power and by Your outstretched arm! Nothing is too difficult for You! I know I can put my trust in You, and in You alone.

But what about our heart?

> *The heart is deceitful above all things and beyond cure. Who can under-*
> *stand it? "I the Lord search the heart and examine the mind, to reward a*
> *man according to his conduct, according to what his deeds deserve."*
> Jeremiah 17:9–10 NIV

This next portion of scripture is very telling. God knows we are going to face problems and temptations. He knows we are going to get discouraged and depressed to the point of giving up sometimes. People tend to think that Christians are perfect; actually, it is just

---

1. Paul Lee Tan, Encyclopedia of 770 Illustrations: Signs of the Times, Assurance Publishers, 1984

the opposite. We all are sinners saved by grace and we all struggle with things in our lives every day.

The Heart is deceitful and beyond cure! We are never going to be free of sin and temptation until we get to heaven. But the Lord knows our heart; He knows that you are trying and with the help of the Holy Spirit you are doing your best to stay strong. He knows that we are going to fail sometimes, that we are going to fall off that tightrope across the river of life.

But we need to know that He will be there to catch us when we do fall

> *In the same way, the Spirit helps us in our weakness. We do not know what we ought to pray for, but the Spirit himself intercedes for us with groans that words cannot express. And he who searches our hearts knows the mind of the Spirit, because the Spirit intercedes for the saints in accordance with the will of God. And we know that in all things God works for the good of those who love him, who have been called according to his purpose.*
>
> Romans 8:26–28 NIV

Sometimes we get so discouraged that we don't even know how to ask God for help. But that is alright because God knows what we need. The important thing is that we ask! And that we trust Him to show us the way. We have all seen some really big trees get blown over in a storm and it is because they have died inside or they have a weak root system that cannot support them.

When we fail to seek God's help and try to work things out on our own, our spiritual roots start weakening and we take our eyes off God and put them on ourselves. It doesn't take long before we start dying spiritually and a major crisis comes along and knocks us over.

Have you ever tried to walk during a strong wind storm? The wind is so strong you can barely stand up, let alone walk! That is how it feels sometimes in life, but if our roots are deep enough and we are spending time praying before God and reading His word, the One who created the wind can calm the storm in our life.

Are your roots planted along the stream supplied by the Holy Spirit? Or are you out in the desert somewhere, hoping someone will come along and help you?

If you are struggling and are ready to plant deep roots, God is ready to quench your thirst and nourish your soul. All you have to is trust him! Are you ready to let God have total control?

No holding back, I surrender all! I want those deep roots that only trusting him can give me!

NOTHING IS TOO DIFFICULT FOR GOD!

BLESSED NATION

Blessed is the nation whose God is the Lord,

the people he chose for his inheritance.

From heaven the Lord looks down and sees all mankind;

from his dwelling place he watches all who live on earth—

he who forms the hearts of all, who considers everything they do.

No king is saved by the size of his army;

no warrior escapes by his great strength.

A horse is a vain hope for deliverance;

despite all its great strength it cannot save.

But the eyes of the Lord are on those who fear him—

on those whose hope is in his unfailing love,

to deliver them from death and keep them alive in famine.

We wait in hope for the Lord;

he is our help and our shield.

In him our hearts rejoice, for we trust in his holy name.

May your unfailing love rest upon us, O Lord, even as we put our hope in you.

Psalm 33:12–22 NIV84

The United States of America is a blessed nation, in spite of all the terrible things that have happened since 1776 and since the Declaration of Independence was proclaimed. There has been a lot of blood shed and lives lost defending this great nation, and there are those who have attempted to take over and destroy all things that we fight so hard to keep. There is always going to be someone trying to take us over, and our only hope is to trust in the Lord and know that He is always there to push back our enemies. There have always been wars and rumors of wars—since the beginning of time; men trying to take what is not theirs from someone else. God has always taken care of His people wherever in the world they are. There are a lot of scary things happening in the United States and around the world today. We are never going to win by using nuclear weapons and threatening our enemies.

Pray that the hand of God will always be on us and that those in power will seek Him and ask for courage and wisdom from Him. The nation that turns its back on God is a nation on the path of destruction.

BLESSINGS IN TRUSTING

But blessed is the man who trusts in the Lord,
whose confidence is in him.
He will be like a tree planted by the water
that sends out its roots by the stream.
It does not fear when heat comes;
its leaves are always green.
It has no worries in a year of drought
and never fails to bear fruit.
The heart is deceitful above all things
and beyond cure.
Who can understand it?
I the Lord search the heart
and examine the mind,
to reward a man according to his conduct,
according to what his deeds deserve.

Jeremiah 17:7–10 NIV84

Jeremiah said the Lord searches the heart and examines the mind to reward a man according to his conduct.

The Lord knows if you are putting your trust in yourself and in your own resources—or in him. Jesus tells a parable about a rich young ruler who asked what he had to do to get eternal life. Jesus told him to sell everything and follow him. The young man went away sorrowful. Many people today are so busy looking for fulfillment everywhere but in God and they are miserable. Today's economy is in the shape it is in because people have put their trust in things, hoping that a larger house or a newer car or an expensive vacation would make them happy. The Bible doesn't say in the stock market we trust. It says blessed is the nation whose God is the Lord. People are hurting right now, and it is because of greed. It isn't just the people on Wall Street. When the economy crashed and the bottom fell out of the stock market, they had nowhere to go. Where is your trust today. God knows your heart and your mind. Are you proud of where your trust is? Or are you frustrated because your trust isn't where it belongs—and that is in the Lord Jesus Christ. Christ is the only one we can put our trust in. We know He will be there for us when bad things happen. If we put our faith and trust in the Lord, it doesn't matter what happens on Wall Street or anywhere else. God is still on the throne, and he will take care of his people no matter what happens, as long as we put our faith and our trust in him. It doesn't matter how much money you have or how big a house you live in, the only thing that matters is that you have put your faith and trust in Jesus Christ.

BREAD OF LIFE

So when the crowd saw that neither Jesus nor his disciples were there, they got into the boats and went across to Capernaum to look for him. They found him on the other side of the lake and asked, "Rabbi, when did you get here?"

Jesus replied, "I tell you the truth, you want to be with me because I fed you, not because you understood the miraculous signs. But don't be so concerned about perishable things like food. Spend your energy seeking the eternal life that the Son of Man can give you. For God the Father has given me the seal of his approval."

They replied, "We want to perform God's works, too. What should we do?"

Jesus told them, "This is the only work God wants from you: Believe in the one he has sent."

They answered, "Show us a miraculous sign if you want us to believe in you. What can you do? After all, our ancestors ate manna while they journeyed through the wilderness! The Scriptures say, 'Moses gave them bread from heaven to eat.'"

Jesus said, "I tell you the truth, Moses didn't give you bread from heaven. My Father did. And now he offers you the true bread from heaven. The true bread of God is the one who comes down from heaven and gives life to the world."

John 6:24–33 NLT

The day before, Jesus had just fed five thousand people with the five barley loaves and two fishes. These were very small loaves of bread and sardine-like fishes. The people had responded by saying, "Surely he is the prophet we have been expecting." But Jesus saw that they were ready to take him by force and make him king, so he went higher into the hills alone, only to be found the next day by them in Capernaum.

He saw through their motives: They wanted him for their own purposes, not because he was the Messiah: "I tell you the truth, you want to be with me because I fed you, not because you understood the miraculous signs." He told them they needed to be concerned about eternal things, not the perishable things of this life, like food. In verse 28, they asked, "What does God want us to do?" Jesus told them this is what God wants you to do: "Believe in the one He has sent." **What was their reply in verse 30?** You must show us a miraculous sign if you want us to believe in you. What will you do for us?

Jesus had just performed a miracle by feeding them with very little food, yet that wasn't enough. They didn't consider that a real miracle! Now manna from heaven, that was a miracle. People are the same way today. God can perform miraculous things in people's lives, yet they refuse to believe He is the one true God. Miracles alone will not save people; they have to truly believe Jesus is who he says he is. The people wanted to use Jesus for their own selfish motives. People still ask God for all kinds of things and make a lot of promises to God if He will answer their prayer. Sometimes God will answer a prayer in a miraculous manner, and people will still turn away from Him and go back to their own way of living. Living for Christ is more than just an outward sign, it is an inward, life changing, Holy Spirit-driven experience that makes you want to live for Him. Not for what He can do for you, but for what you can do for Him. Jesus said you don't believe in me, even though you have seen me. If you are going to believe in miracles, you have to believe in a God of miracles. If you don't believe Jesus is the Son of God, you aren't going to believe anything He does and be skeptical of anything that happens in the name of Jesus. They are maybe once or twice in a lifetime events. A parking space in the Walmart parking lot at Christmas time isn't a miracle, even though it seems like it. A miracle is something that cannot be explained any other way than by the Grace of God. I f you believe in the inerrancy of scripture, then you have to believe in miracles.

BREAKTHROUGH

> O they will break through the gate and go out.
> Their king will pass through before them,
> the Lord at their head."
>
> Micah 2:13 NIV84

Chuck Yeager was a World War II hero who broke the sound barrier. Everybody who had tried it before had gotten to a certain speed, and the plane would start shaking so violently that it seemed as if it was going to disintegrate. Some of the planes did disintegrate and the pilots died. In other words, experience showed that it couldn't be done. But twenty-four-year-old Chuck wanted to try it anyway.

Right before his flight in October of 1947, he broke two of his ribs in a horseback riding accident and was in extreme pain. People said he shouldn't go up. He wondered if his body was capable of handling the extreme stress, but he decided to try it anyway. He said at seven hundred miles an hour the plane began to shake violently, but then he broke through into a great calm.

That is how it is when you are about to get a breakthrough: Everything around you starts shaking and falling apart. Everything is going crazy; you feel as if your whole world is falling to pieces. Satan starts hammering you and you start thinking, "I can't do this." That doesn't mean you are going to crash and burn. God is faithful to finish what he has started. Like Chuck Yeager, we need to find a way to break through our problems into the next level of victory. If you are in a shaky situation right now, don't give up. You are just on the other side of a great calm. The key to breaking through is to break out and go for it. You have to be able to say, "I don't care about the past, I don't care what other people think, I know God has given me a promise." You need to break out in your own mind and your own faith in order to pave the way for a breakthrough. The Lord will go before and open the gate so you can break out; all you have to do is walk through the gate of opportunity, the gate of grace, the gate of forgiveness. Break out of self-imposed limitations. Break out of negative thinking. Break out of fear. Break out of past failures. Break out of depression and hopelessness. Break out of the bondage of addictions.

Jesus said he would never forsake you if you have the faith to believe He can deliver from your addiction. He will—all you have to do is ask. With His help all things are possible.

CALLING ON GOD

In the day when I cried out, You answered me,
And made me bold with strength in my soul.
All the kings of the earth shall praise You, O Lord,
When they hear the words of Your mouth.

Psalm 138:3–4 NKJV

Are you crying out for help and it seems nobody is listening? God is listening and he will answer you; all you have to do is ask. His wisdom is greater than all the kings and leaders in the world. He will never give you bad advice and he will give you the strength to carry on when you feel like giving up. Try calling on the one who made you and knows all about you. You won't regret it.

CHOICES

> *A wise person chooses the right road;*
> *a fool takes the wrong one.*
>
> Ecclesiastes 10:2 NLT

There has been a lot of discussion lately about the possibility of the government mandating everyone to get the COVID 19 vaccine. God clearly gives people the right to choose or reject him. Noah and the Ark comes to mind. Everyone laughed at Noah until it started raining and didn't stop. We all make choices every day and the wise person prays that God will give them wisdom to make the right choice.

I know that I have been the fool taking the wrong road when I didn't pray first and ask God what I should do. Whether it is getting a vaccine, or making a major decision in your life, ask God to help you make the right choice.

CHRIST IS OUR CONQUEROR

> *For this reason I bow my knees to the Father of our Lord Jesus Christ, from whom the whole family in heaven and earth is named, that He would grant you, according to the riches of His glory, to be strengthened with might through His Spirit the inner man, that Christ may dwell in your hearts through faith; that you, being rooted and grounded in love, may be able to comprehend with all the saints what is the width and length and depth and height—to know the love of Christ which passes knowledge; that you may be filled with all the fullness of God. Now to Him who is able to do exceedingly abundantly above all that we ask or think, according to the power that works in us, to Him be glory in the church by Christ Jesus to all generations, forever and ever. Amen.*
>
> Ephesians 3:14–21 NKJV

It is the power of the Holy Spirit living and dwelling within us that gives us the strength and power to do things and ask for things in his name. Think about what Paul said: He can do more than we can ask or imagine! That means that what God wants to do for us is beyond our wildest dreams!

If our spirit is in tune with His spirit, nothing is impossible with God. Stop thinking and living in the flesh and start living in the Spirit. Our flesh is dying and that is what kills us spiritually. It is only when we live in the spirit that we truly live. "For in Him we live and move and have our being, as also some of your own poets have said, 'For we are His offspring'" (Acts 17:28–29 NKJV).

It is time to die to self and start living in the Spirit!

COMFORT FOR MY SOUL

> *In the multitude of my anxieties within me, Your comforts delight my soul.*
>
> Psalm 94:19 NKJV

The Bible talks a lot about people getting into situations where they are very anxious, and they don't know what to do. The servants in the fiery furnace and Daniel in The Lions Den are just two examples of many times when God intervened.

We all find ourselves in situations where we have to pray that God will help us, because there is no other way out. Sometimes we don't know what to do, and that is where the Holy Spirit intervenes and speaks to us in that still, small voice, telling us to listen to what God is trying to say. If you are stubborn like me, it takes the Holy Spirit talking to us a few times for God to get His message across. Anxiety is nothing to be ashamed of; we all have to turn to God sometimes and ask for help—and maybe even repent for ignoring Him. Once we do, there is a peace that comes over us that is like no other and we know that everything is going to be alright. Maybe you are fighting a battle right now and have tried everything. Maybe it is time to get on your knees and give your troubles to God. He will give the help and comfort you are looking for.

COMPLACENCY IS A DANGEROUS THING

We are being lulled into a false sense of security today, just as people were in Jesus' day. People were living the good life, thinking the government had it all under control and there would be peace, love and joy in the city, and everything was good. Jesus knew that political power and the motives of men can only lead to destruction. Many times throughout history, people have gotten complacent and destruction was the result. World War I was called the war to end all wars, and during the 1920's, people became complacent and indulged in every luxury and sinful pleasure known to man. They became rich and America was prosperous; life was good and a never-ending party. Then came the stock market crash of 1929. People were standing in line for food and barely surviving; once rich and powerful men who had been consumed by greed were committing suicide because their fortunes were gone and they had placed all of their trust in their money instead of God. Then came World War II and massive casualties all over the entire world because of the power and greed of a few men who wanted to rule the world. I don't think there has ever been a time of peace in the world where all nations were working together for the common good and nobody was at war. People keep talking about world peace, but they are very poor historians and very naïve if they really think there is ever going to be true peace in the world before the return of Christ. Until Satan is conquered and thrown into the lake of fire, there is always going to be discord in this world—because that is what Satan does. He lulls us into a false sense of security. The moment we let our guard down, he will be right there to wreak havoc and destruction. Be alert and ready for Christ's return because it could happen at any time, and those who have gotten lazy and complacent will be left behind.

CONTENTMENT

> *I rejoice greatly in the Lord that at last you have renewed your concern for me. Indeed, you have been concerned, but you had no opportunity to show it. I am not saying this because I am in need, for I have learned to be content whatever the circumstances. I know what it is to be in need, and I know what it is to have plenty. I have learned the secret of being content in any and every situation, whether well fed or hungry, whether living in plenty or in want. I can do everything through him who gives me strength.*
>
> Philippians 4:10–13 NIV

Paul had learned the secret of contentment, and it wasn't anything the world had provided him. He was grateful for the things that people had sent him, but even without those things he knew his strength and his rest came from the Lord. Paul was a man who had known wealth and privilege, and he realized those things did not bring him happiness, because those things are only temporary. Our outward circumstances are constantly changing and we cannot depend on those things. People gain and lose fortunes every day; people lose their homes through earthquakes, fires and hurricanes. People lose loved ones through sickness and death, but the one constant we have in our lives is God.

COURAGE

> *Be strong and courageous, because you will lead these people to inherit the land I swore to their forefathers to give them. Be strong and very courageous. Be careful to obey all the law my servant Moses gave you; do not turn from it to the right or to the left, that you may be successful wherever you go. Do not let this Book of the Law depart from your mouth; meditate on it day and night, so that you may be careful to do everything written in it. Then you will be prosperous and successful. Have I not commanded you? Be strong and courageous. Do not be terrified; do not be discouraged, for the Lord your God will be with you wherever you go.*
>
> Joshua 1:6–9 NIV84

God told Joshua three times in this passage of scripture to be strong and courageous. Joshua was about to lead the people into the Promised Land, and he knew there would be tough times ahead. He knew what Moses had gone through, with the people rebelling and disobeying God. He also knew that only by obeying God and His word would he be successful. Being courageous in a tough situation is hard to do sometimes.

A lot of times it seems like it would be easier to run from the problem than face it. People spend their entire lives running from their problems. But there always comes a time when you have to stand and face your problems. Some of you are facing some very difficult situations in your life. In verse 9, God said "Do not be discouraged, for the Lord your God will be with you wherever you go." Sometimes when things go wrong, people mistakenly think God has deserted them and they start blaming Him. That could not be further from the truth; sometimes it is our own disobedience that causes our problems. The Children of Israel were disobedient to God, but He was still there, and He still looked after them in spite of their own stubbornness. It wasn't God who rebelled and refused to listen. It wasn't God who started worshiping idols. Joshua faced a very tough situation and was ultimately successful because he listened to God and did exactly what God told him. Joshua was probably one of the strongest and most courageous men in the Bible, being able to finally lead the Children of Israel into their promised land—all because he was obedient to God.

DAY OF REST

> *The sabbath was made for man and not man for the sabbath.*
>
> Mark 2:27 NIV

When God declared that one day of the week be declared a day of sabbath, He did it for our own good. The sabbath was meant to be a day of rest, prayer, and worshiping God. It was very strictly enforced, sometimes too strictly. Even God took a day off when he created the universe. Sometimes we get so busy doing what we think is important, we almost kill ourselves trying get it done. I have heard people say, "I will rest when I am dead." No you won't! You will be dead and whatever was so important will still be there, left undone. We keep the doctors and hospitals in business because we refuse to take the time to rest, relax and enjoy this wonderful world that God gave us to enjoy.

Whether you attend the church of your choice, spend time with family or just rest, do yourself a favor and take a day to enjoy what the Lord has blessed you with.

DEATH IS NOTHING TO FEAR

> *For this perishable body must put on the imperishable, this mortal body must put on immortality. When the perishable puts on the imperishable, and the mortal puts on immortality, then shall come to pass the saying that is written:*
> *"Death is swallowed up in victory.*
> *O death, where is your victory? O death, where is your sting?"*
> *The sting of death is sin, and the power of sin is the law. But thanks be to God, who gives us the victory through our Lord Jesus Christ.*
>
> 1 Corinthians 16:53–57 ESV

Most people don't fear death, but fear where they are going. As a chaplain and pastor, I sat with many people who were passing away. I always could tell who knew the Lord. They died very peacefully and knew they were assured a place in heaven. My father was very devoted to the Lord. When he was dying, he was unconscious and suddenly he sat up in bed and raised his arms and his eyes toward heaven and motioned toward heaven as if motioning someone to come get him. Then he laid back down and never moved again. He died later that night. I don't know who he saw, but I know he is in heaven today. If you haven't accepted Jesus as your savior, do it now before it is too late, and death will turn into victory.

DESIRE FOR GOD

> *Whom have I in heaven but you?*
> *And earth has nothing I desire besides you.*
> *My flesh and my heart may fail,*
> *but God is the strength of my heart*
> *and my portion forever.*
>
> Psalm 73:25–26 NIV84

Human desires will come and go, and our health will eventually fail us. God will always be there and, if we put our desire for him above everything else, when all else fails and we have nothing left but God, he will still be there waiting patiently for us to come home to be with him.

DO-OVERS

> *Then Jesus, again groaning in Himself, came to the tomb. It was a cave, and a stone lay against it. Jesus said, "Take away the stone." Martha, the sister of him who was dead, said to Him, "Lord, by this time there is a stench, for he has been dead four days." Jesus said to her, "Did I not say to you that if you would believe you would see the glory of God?" Then they took away the stone from the place where the dead man was lying. And Jesus lifted up His eyes and said, "Father, I thank You that You have heard Me. And I know that You always hear Me, but because of the people who are standing by I said this, that they may believe that You sent Me." Now when He had said these things, He cried with a loud voice, "Lazarus, come forth!" And he who had died came out bound hand and foot with graveclothes, and his face was wrapped with a cloth. Jesus said to them, "Loose him, and let him go."*
>
> John 11:38–44 NKJV

Have you ever thought about how you would live your life if you got a do-over? I have, but there are no guarantees I would have more success—in fact I could do worse.

The only person I know of that got a do-over of sorts is Lazarus, the brother of Mary and Martha. We don't know anything about his life after he was resurrected by Jesus. He didn't write a book telling what heaven was like and go on the speaking circuit. I would like to think that Lazarus told everyone he knew what Jesus had done for him.

Alas, there are no do-overs, but we can tell everyone what Jesus has done for us and how our life has changed since we asked forgiveness for our sins. The point is, we don't have to die to have a new life. All we need is Jesus. His grace covers all of our sins and gives us a fresh start.

DON'T BE A JONAH

> *Then some of the Pharisees and teachers of the law said to him, "Teacher, we want to see a miraculous sign from you." He answered, "A wicked and adulterous generation asks for a miraculous sign! But none will be given it except the sign of the prophet Jonah. For as Jonah was three days and three nights in the belly of a huge fish, so the Son of Man will be three days and three nights in the heart of the earth."*
>
> Matthew 12:38–40 NIV

By saying the people would only receive the sign of Jonah, Jesus is pointing out that, just as Jonah was three nights in a huge fish, so Jesus would be in the tomb three nights.

Jonah was a good prophet (see 2 Kings 14:25); that is, until he refused to go to Nineveh because he hated the Ninevites. He kept running from God until he got thrown over board during a violent storm and immediately the waters calmed and the storm stopped. Jonah had three days in the belly of a fish to contemplate how he had wound up there and what he was going to do if he got out.

All of us have some form of Jonah in us and refuse or try to bargain with God because we don't want to do something the Lord wants us to do. Some people run for a long time and it takes something drastic for them to realize you can't run from God. He will always engineer a plan to get us to turn back to Him and do His will. If you feel God is telling you to do something, spend some time in prayer asking for Him to show you what it is you are to do. He will lead the way, all you have to do is follow and be obedient to His will.

SO DON'T BE A JONAH! You will never regret following Christ and doing his will.

DOUBT

"The main problem with doubting God is not what it does to us, but what it keeps us from doing."

Faith and Doubt, John Ortberg

Consider it pure joy, my brothers and sisters, whenever you face trials of many kinds, because you know that the testing of your faith produces perseverance. Let perseverance finish its work so that you may be mature and complete, not lacking anything. If any of you lacks wisdom, you should ask God, who gives generously to all without finding fault, and it will be given to you. But when you ask, you must believe and not doubt, because the one who doubts is like a wave of the sea, blown and tossed by the wind. That person should not expect to receive anything from the Lord. Such a person is double-minded and unstable in all they do. Believers in humble circumstances ought to take pride in their high position.

James 1:2–9 NIV

We are all going to have problems, and things happen sometimes that test our faith. We have to remember the Bible tells us that things are going to happen. Christ suffered all kinds of trials and persecutions when he was here on earth, so what makes us think that we won't? Are we better than Christ? Do we really expect to go through life and everything be perfect all the time? If you do, you're delusional, because that's not what life is about. Life in your Christian walk is a journey; the farther you go, and the more you persevere, the more you grow. God understands us, and if we ask him, he will give us wisdom to be able to get through the tough times in our lives. It is only by having faith and trust in God to see you through that we can. The one thing he asked us not to do is doubt, because doubt will cause us to stray from God, and start looking at other ways to satisfy our needs, and that always leads to trouble. James says anyone who doubts God after putting their trust in him is double minded and unstable in all that he does. We should never look anywhere else but to God for help.

> *I say this because many deceivers, who do not acknowledge Jesus Christ as coming in the flesh, have gone out into the world. Any such person is the deceiver and the antichrist. Watch out that you do not lose what we have worked for, but that you may be rewarded fully. Anyone who runs ahead and does not continue in the teaching of Christ does not have God; whoever continues in the teaching has both the Father and the Son. If anyone comes to you and does not bring this teaching, do not take them into your house or welcome them. Anyone who welcomes them shares in their wicked work.*
>
> 2 John 1:7–11 NIV

Many people have heard the message of the gospel and rejected it only to embrace some other guy that they think will help them better. Anyone who turns away from God will find it much harder in the end, because they knew the truth of Christ's message and rejected him. The Bible tells us that it will be better for those who never heard the gospel then for those who who have and rejected it. Satan is very smart and cunning. He makes sin and all the things the world has to offer seem very attractive. He knows the Bible better than you do, and he will try to use it against you to make you doubt that it's true, just like he did with Adam and Eve.

ENCOURAGING EACH OTHER

> *Let us hold tightly without wavering to the hope we affirm, for God can be trusted to keep his promise. Let us think of ways to motivate one another to acts of love and good works. And let us not neglect our meeting together, as some people do, but encourage one another, especially now that the day of his return is drawing near.*
>
> Hebrews 10:23–25 NLT

If you went to church this morning, it doesn't matter where you went. As the book of Hebrews tells us, the purpose is to meet together and to encourage each other in our faith through Jesus Christ. Some people like to praise God through raising their hands and speaking in tongues. Others prefer sitting in quiet reverence before God and worshiping Him. The important thing is to worship our Lord and Savior Jesus Christ, especially in these perilous times when people are rejecting God and Christianity. It is more important than ever to draw closer to God and each other as the time of His return is drawing near.

May God's blessings be upon you.

ENJOY THE DAY

> *Rejoice in the Lord always. Again I will say, rejoice! Let your gentleness be known to all men.... Be anxious for nothing, but in everything, by prayer and supplication,... let your requests be made known to God; and the peace of God, which surpasses all understanding, will guard your hearts and minds through Christ Jesus.*
>
> Philippians 4:4–7 NKJV

Someone once said, "Until the Lord opens the door, praise him in the hallway." Sometimes we get so anxious worrying about what is going to happen next we forget to live in the present. Jesus said, don't worry about tomorrow, today has enough troubles of its own (Matthew 6:34). Today may be all we have and we should enjoy it; nobody is promised tomorrow. I thank the Lord every morning for the day he has given me.

The Anxiety and Depression Association of America (ADAA) reports that Social Anxiety Disorder alone affects 15 million adults in the US (7.1% of the population).[1] It is equally common among men and women.

---

1. "Facts & Statistics," Anxiety & Depression Association of America, last modified Jun 27, 2022, https://adaa.org/understanding-anxiety/facts-statistics

These statistics on Social Anxiety Disorder are very troubling. They include a whole range of mental health problems. We live in the richest and most prosperous country in the world, yet people get so depressed, some take their own lives out of despair.

The only permanent cure for all these things is to accept Jesus Christ as your savior. Most of the treatment programs available work temporarily and then people are in the same depressed state they were in before.

Everyone gets sad and depressed at times, but Jesus said, "be anxious for nothing." Jesus can and does heal people having mental health issues. The secret is to talk to Him daily and study His Word. Most importantly, give your problems to Him and He will help you get through whatever you are going through today. Talk to Dr. Jesus. His door is always open; you don't have to make an appointment—He is willing to listen to you any time.

My prayer for you is that you have a blessed day and enjoy every minute of it. It is a great day to be alive, giving God all the glory.

ENLARGE MY TERRITORY

> *And Jabez called on the God of Israel saying, "Oh, that You would bless me indeed, and enlarge my territory, that Your hand would be with me, and that You would keep me from evil, that I may not cause pain!" So God granted him what he requested.*
>
> 1 Chronicles 4:10 NKJV

You may be very successful without knowing the Lord, but it is oh so much sweeter when the hand of the Lord is on you, and he is blessing you with more than you ever could achieve by yourself. God loves his children and gives them his blessing in many ways.

Jabez was a righteous man who called out to the Lord and asked for his blessing that he may be faithful and not sin against God. When you trust God with your life, God will bless you more than you could ever imagine. God truly does love His children and shows His love in many different ways. We cannot out-give or out-love God. Jabez' prayer was simple and honest, and God answered his prayer in ways that Jabez never imagined. Give it all to God. He loves you and wants to show you His love every day.

EVERY ONE OF US CAN DO SOMETHING

Whether it is answering the phone and referring that person to someone who can help them.

Whether it is calling someone and making sure they are safe and don't need any help.

Whether it is going to someone's house and visiting with them.

Whether it is picking up someone's mail.

Whether it is driving someone to a doctor's appointment.

Just simply being someone's friend is the most precious thing we can do.

These acts open up opportunities to share Christ, which can make all the difference in the world.

Do something for someone else. You will be surprised how good it will make you feel.

FAILURE

As Jesus walked beside the Sea of Galilee, he saw Simon and his brother Andrew casting a net into the lake, for they were fishermen. "Come, follow me," Jesus said, "and I will send you out to fish for people." At once they left their nets and followed him. When he had gone a little farther, he saw James son of Zebedee and his brother John in a boat, preparing their nets. Without delay he called them, and they left their father Zebedee in the boat with the hired men and followed him.

Mark 1:16–20 NIV

Sometimes I feel like a total failure and that God could never use someone like me for anything. Then I remember there were twelve guys who followed Jesus around that were full of bravado as long as Jesus was around. The disciples were just ordinary men who had no training or education. They were mostly laborers and fishermen. When Jesus told them to follow Him, they followed Him with an incredible amount of faith. The Pharisees scoffed at their lack of education. But, when He needed them most, they all ran away and hid. They were all failures! They had to learn that their strength and courage came from Jesus, not themselves. It took Jesus' death on the cross and His resurrection for them to realize that their strength came from Him, not themselves. Even Judas learned a very hard lesson about taking his eyes off Jesus and trusting others for his reward. Romans 3:23

says we all have sinned and fell short of the glory of God. God will use you where you are; it doesn't matter what you have done. All you have to do is put your trust in Him and not yourself. Many of us are just like the disciples, trying to do things our way instead of trusting God and having the faith to follow him, not knowing what the future holds, but trusting the one who holds the future. Who have you put your faith in, yourself or the one who can make you and mold you into the person He wants you to be?

FAITH WITHOUT JESUS

When they came to the crowd, a man approached Jesus and knelt before him. "Lord, have mercy on my son," he said. "He has seizures and is suffering greatly. He often falls into the fire or into the water. I brought him to your disciples, but they could not heal him."

"O unbelieving and perverse generation," Jesus replied, "how long shall I stay with you? How long shall I put up with you? Bring the boy here to me."

Jesus rebuked the demon, and it came out of the boy, and he was healed from that moment. Then the disciples came to Jesus in private and asked, "Why couldn't we drive it out?" He replied, "Because you have so little faith. I tell you the truth, if you have faith as small as a mustard seed, you can say to this mountain, 'Move from here to there' and it will move. Nothing will be impossible for you."

Matthew 17:14–22 NIV84

The disciples were trying to drive out the demon on their own, but they hadn't realized that it is only by the power in the name of Jesus we can do anything. Our power, our strength, our courage comes from God; if we fail to pray and seek God before we attempt anything, we are doomed to failure before we start. Joshua knew this; he knew that only by being obedient to God was he going to be successful. Do you think that if it had been

Joshua's idea to march around Jericho seven times the walls would have fallen? Joshua never went into battle without God directing him as to what to do and where to go. We all fight spiritual battles every day of our lives, and it is only by the power of God that we can stay strong. There are so many hurting people in the world today that need to realize the simple fact that only by trusting in God will they have peace of mind and the courage to do what is right in their lives. We are living in a time when people are losing hope and getting desperate about how they are going to survive. Only by faith in God and knowing He holds the future can we survive in a dark and sinful world.

FEAR NOT

Franklin D Roosevelt's first inaugural address, March 4, 1933:

I am certain that my fellow Americans expect that on my induction into the Presidency I will address them with a candor and a decision which the present situation of our people impels. This is preeminently the time to speak the truth, the whole truth, frankly and boldly. Nor need we shrink from honestly facing conditions in our country today. This great Nation will endure as it has endured, will revive and will prosper. So, first of all, let me assert my firm belief that the only thing we have to fear is fear itself—nameless, unreasoning, unjustified terror which paralyzes needed efforts to convert retreat into advance. In every dark hour of our national life a leadership of frankness and vigor has met with that understanding and support of the people themselves which is essential to victory. I am convinced that you will again give that support to leadership in these critical days.

President Roosevelt was right about fear being paralyzing and causing people to do nothing instead of fighting through fear and conquering the enemy within us. The Bible says "fear not" 365 times! I think God is trying to tell us something. Jesus himself said, "Fear not for I have overcome the world."

> *Be anxious for nothing, but in everything by prayer and supplication, with*
> *thanksgiving, let your requests be made known to God.*
>
> Philippians 4:6 NKJV

This nation has been through a lot of terrible times and came back stronger than ever. Do not let all the people trying to spread fear and destroy this nation cause you to be fearful. This too shall pass, and this nation will be stronger than ever. Jesus has already conquered fear and sin and death. There are always going to be things happening that will make us anxious and fearful. That is part of life and will be until Christ Returns to this earth. He said he would never leave us or forsake us.

So, fear not and rejoice, just put your trust in God and He will do the rest.

FELLOWSHIP IS THE LIFEBLOOD

> That which was from the beginning, which we have heard, which we have seen with our eyes, which we have looked at and our hands have touched — this we proclaim concerning the Word of life. The life appeared; we have seen it and testify to it, and we proclaim to you the eternal life, which was with the Father and has appeared to us. We proclaim to you what we have seen and heard, so that you also may have fellowship with us. And our fellowship is with the Father and with his Son, Jesus Christ. We write this to make our joy complete.
>
> If we confess our sins, he is faithful and just and will forgive us our sins and purify us from all unrighteousness. If we claim we have not sinned, we make him out to be a liar and his word is not in us.
>
> 1 John 1:1–4,9–10 NIV

Most churches have many programs intended to reach as many people as possible. The trick is to make that fellowship meaningful and not be just a time of socializing. What happens on Sunday morning depends on what the church does during the week. If people are fellowshipping with and worshiping God during the week, that is going to spill over on Sunday morning because people are going to come to church with a sense of expectancy and be excited about what the Holy Spirit is going to do during the service. That is why there are small groups, Bible studies and midweek services—to help people worship God during the week and stay connected.

Do you come to church expecting to hear from God and to fellowship with him on Sunday morning?

LISTEN TO THIS ANALOGY BETWEEN A CHURCH AND A BAR

The neighborhood bar is possibly the best counterfeit there is to the fellowship Christ wants to give his church. It's an imitation, dispensing liquor instead of grace, escape rather than reality, but it is a permissive, accepting and inclusive fellowship. It is unshockable. It is democratic. You can tell people secrets and they usually don't tell others or even want to. The bar flourishes not because most people are alcoholics, but because God has put into the human heart the desire to know and be known, to love and be loved, and so many seek a counterfeit at the price of a few beers.

With all my heart I believe that Christ wants his church to be unshockable, democratic, permissive-a fellowship where people can come in and say,

"I'm sunk!" "I'm beat!" "I've had it" Alcoholics Anonymous has this quality. Our churches too often miss it.[1]

All too often the church is exclusive instead of inclusive. People don't feel welcome when they walk in the door—and that is sad. The church should be a welcoming place where people find fellowship and help; finding answers to the problems they are facing. Just like one of the most famous bars in television history, it should be "A place where everybody knows your name."

Prayer, teaching and fellowship all add up to a church being totally surrendered to God's will, expecting God to do great things in the church.

Philippians 4:13 says *"I can do everything through Christ who gives me strength."* And we can, as long we remain in fellowship with Him and His will for our lives

---

1. Edge of Adventure: An Experiment in Faith, Miller and Larson, Word, 1975

FELLOWSHIP WITH GOD

> *Therefore go and make disciples of all nations, baptizing them in the name of the Father and of the Son and of the Holy Spirit, and teaching them to obey everything I have commanded you. And surely I am with you always, to the very end of the age.*
>
> Matthew 28:19–20 NIV

Fellowship with God is the first rule of fellowship. That is why the foundations of prayer and teaching are so important. The reason the church exists is to worship and have fellowship with God. If our hearts and minds aren't in fellowship with God, then God isn't the head of the church. We are placing ourselves and our own desires above what God would have us do.

Christ gave a very stern warning to churches that get too comfortable and aren't constantly seeking to have fellowship with God, seeking Him above all things. It doesn't say make disciples of all the people that you like, and you want to be part of the church, it says all people. Fellowship starts in the heart of the believer and extends to the people around you. If we are not attracting new people into this fellowship, then we are doing something wrong.

But if anyone obeys his word, God's love is truly made complete in him. This is how we know we are in him: Whoever claims to live in him must walk as Jesus did.

1 John 2:5–6 NIV84

Do you see what John says? We must walk as Jesus did. Those are some pretty big sandals to fill. What did Jesus do? He met people's needs and ministered to them both physically and spiritually. In Revelation 3:20, He says He is standing at the door of people's hearts and knocking, waiting to be invited in. It is the job of churches to help people open the door of their hearts and let Christ through His Holy Spirit come in and fellowship with them. Whenever you fellowship with someone, it is because you like them and enjoy being around them. The church should be a place where people enjoy coming and enjoy fellowshipping with God and the people of the church. That is why churches usually have several different types of programs to offer, in order to reach as many people as possible. The trick is to make that fellowship meaningful and not just a time of socializing. What happens on Sunday morning depends on what the church does during the week. If people are fellowshipping with and worshiping God during the week, that is going to spill over on Sunday morning, because people are going to come to church with a sense of expectancy, excited about what the Holy Spirit is going to do during the service.

The main thing which many people forget is the people are the church. It isn't a brick-and-mortar building. What each us do during the week represents the church. Our bodies are the temple of the Holy Spirit. We should be fellowshipping with God all week and setting a Christ like example for everyone. You are the church and what you do matters more than you may realize.

FINISHING THE RACE

> *But one thing I do: Forgetting what is behind and straining toward what is ahead, I press on toward the goal to win the prize for which God has called me heavenward in Christ Jesus.*
>
> Philippians 3:13–14 NIV

We all have things in our past that we wish we could forget. Even though we know that Christ has forgiven us and he has washed our sins away, never to be remembered by Him ever again. We tend to be our own worst enemy when trying to forget the past and move on with the future. Satan likes to remind us of our past and try to make us feel guilty about those things which Christ has already forgotten. Our past is always going to be there and we can't go back and live our lives over again. Sitting around and playing the "what if" game only makes things worse. What if I had made different choices or made better decisions? What if I had not married the person I did? What if I had chosen a different career?

The apostle Paul had a very checkered past and had the lives of many Christians on his hands, until he was personally spoken to by Jesus on the Damascus road. He was able to put his past behind him and became one of the most ardent followers of Jesus Christ, even writing most of the New Testament. We have to do what Paul recommends and keep looking forward to finishing the race that we are running, the race called life.

Take those things from the past and use them against Satan, reminding him that you are forgiven and he no longer has any power over you. You can help others come to Christ by helping them ask Christ to forgive them of their past and that a glorious future awaits. Christ is waiting for them to ask and he will forgive. It is that simple. If you haven't asked Jesus into your heart, do it today. If you have, find someone you can help lead to Christ so they too can forget their past. And look with rejoicing toward their future.

FIRST THINGS FIRST

> *But seek first his kingdom and his righteousness, and all these things will be given to you as well. Therefore do not worry about tomorrow, for tomorrow will worry about itself. Each day has enough trouble of its own.*
>
> Matthew 6:33–34 NIV

If you start putting God first in your life and start trusting him for your needs, He will make sure you have everything you need. He knows what you need before you even ask Him. So quit worrying and start trusting God for your needs. He is just waiting on you!

Sometimes it can be very difficult to trust God and give everything to Him, even though we know that is what we should do. But in our minds we think that we can conquer our problems on our own without God's help. That is when we start worrying and become anxious. By trying to do things on our own, we open the door for Satan to try and convince us that we don't need God. Give it all to God every day and let *Him* give you the peace of knowing He is going to take care of you and whatever the future may hold.

FOOLISH WISDOM

> *For the message of the cross is foolishness to those who are perishing, but to us who are being saved it is the power of God. For it is written: "I will destroy the wisdom of the wise, And bring to nothing the understanding of the prudent." Where is the wise? Where is the scribe? Where is the disputer of this age? Has not God made foolish the wisdom of this world?*
>
> 1 Corinthians 1:18–20 NKJV

God can use bad people and bad situations for His glory. The conflict between Jacob and Esau, and the death of Jesus Christ are just two examples. Even today, God can take bad situations and use them for his glory. We look around us and see all the bad things that are happening in the world, and even in our own lives, and we start getting anxious and upset. Then we take things in our own hands and often make things worse.

God has a huge advantage over the rest of us: He knows what the results of our actions are going to be; He knows what is going to happen in the future. He can take our lemons and make them into lemonade. Wouldn't it be wonderful if everybody looked to God for advice before making a decision? We could save ourselves so much heartache and trouble. Believe me, I have made a lot of bad decisions in my life and if I would have asked God first and waited for an answer, instead of blundering my way forward, I would have saved myself a lot of grief and time.

Will you make up your mind today that you are going to trust God with the decisions you make, no matter how important or seemingly insignificant? Nothing going on in our lives is too small for God to help us with, but we have to be willing to let him. God doesn't go where he is not wanted. So the next time you make a decision, go to God first and make it a matter of prayer. You will be glad you did. You will look like a very wise person instead of a fool.

Do you see a man wise in his own eyes?
There is more hope for a fool than for him.

Proverbs 26:12 NKJV

FORGIVEN AND FORGOTTEN

> *See, I will create new heavens and a new earth. The former things will not be remembered, nor will they come to mind. But be glad and rejoice forever in what I will create, for I will create Jerusalem to be a delight and its people a joy. I will rejoice over Jerusalem and take delight in my people; the sound of weeping and of crying will be heard in it no more.*
>
> Isaiah 65:17-19 NIV

Someday all of the heartbreak and the evil things of this world will be gone. We will be new creations in Christ Jesus and reign with Him forever. What a glorious day that will be when we will be able to rejoice with Him and experience the peace and joy that we all long for forever and ever. Amen!

GIVING IS A BLESSING

> *You yourselves know that these hands of mine have supplied my own needs and the needs of my companions. In everything I did, I showed you that by this kind of hard work we must help the weak, remembering the words the Lord Jesus himself said: "It is more blessed to give than to receive."*
>
> Acts 20:34–35 NIV

You have probably heard the saying of Jesus, "It is more blessed to give than to receive." Paul quotes it in the scripture above, and then explains how he lived it by example by only keeping what he needed for himself and giving any extra to those who were in need.

I can honestly say that over years this simple word of knowledge by Jesus has been proven true in my wife Kathy's and my life. We were skeptical at first when we started giving our tithe, because we had bills to pay with that money. But sure enough, every month we paid our tithe and the money always came from somewhere to pay our bills. We have given substantial amounts of money through the years that were over and above our tithe. We have always been blessed in one way or another. The bills have always been paid and God has been glorified.

There is another saying: "You can't out give the Lord." The Lord loves His children, and He wants the best for them. I am not talking about the prosperity gospel or giving all of your money to the church and expecting them to take care of you. It's just a simple principle of giving your tithe faithfully to the church and anything extra that the Lord wants you to give, as you pray about it and feel prompted by Holy Spirit to do. This can be a very controversial subject, and there are those who would abuse this simple command by the Lord. Before you give to any ministry you are not familiar with, always pray about it and get a peace about it from the Lord before you do it.

GOD BLESS AMERICA

Blessed is the nation whose God is the Lord, the people he chose for his inheritance. From heaven the Lord looks down and sees all mankind; from his dwelling place he watches all who live on earth—he who forms the hearts of all, who considers everything they do. No king is saved by the size of his army; no warrior escapes by his great strength. A horse is a vain hope for deliverance; despite all its great strength it cannot save. But the eyes of the Lord are on those who fear him, on those whose hope is in his unfailing love, to deliver them from death and keep them alive in famine. We wait in hope for the Lord; he is our help and our shield. In him our hearts rejoice, for we trust in his holy name. May your unfailing love be with us, Lord, even as we put our hope in you.

Psalm 33:12-22 NIV

Look at these excerpts from the Declaration of Independence:

WHEN in the Course of human Events, it becomes necessary for one People to dissolve the Political Bands which have connected them with another, and to assume among the Powers of the Earth, the separate and equal Station to which the Laws of Nature and of Nature's God entitle them, a decent Respect to the Opinions of Mankind requires that they should declare the causes which impel them to the Separation. We hold these Truths to be self-evident, that all Men are created equal, that they are endowed by their Creator with certain unalienable Rights, that among these are Life, Liberty, and the Pursuit of Happiness...

We, therefore, the Representatives of the UNITED STATES OF AMERICA, in General Congress, Assembled, appealing to the Supreme Judge of the World for the Rectitude of our Intentions, do, in the Name, and by Authority of the good People of these Colonies, solemnly Publish and Declare, That these United Colonies are, and of Right ought to be, Free and Independent States; that they are absolved from all Allegiance to the British Crown, and that all political Connection between them and the State of Great-Britain, is and ought to be totally dissolved; and that as Free and Independent States, they have full Power to levy War, conclude Peace, contract Alliances, establish Commerce, and to do all other Acts and Things which Independent States may of right do. And for the support of this Declaration, with a firm Reliance on the Protection of divine Providence, we mutually pledge to each other our Lives, our Fortunes, and our sacred Honor.

Our founding fathers recognized that God is our creator and he is our protector. They didn't just decide to go to war with Britain on their own. They prayed about it and asked for God's protection and his blessings. This nation was founded by people who were on their knees and praying to God they would be able to start a country were all men were created equal and had equal protections. One of our founding fathers, George Washington, had a few things to say about a godly nation:

It's impossible to govern a nation without God and the Bible. Let us with caution indulge the supposition that morality can be maintained without religion. Reason and experience both forbid us to expect that national morality can prevail in exclusion of religious principle.

Our founding fathers knew that a moral nation is a godly nation. Morals aren't something you're born with, you learn morals as you grow, listen, and watch those around you. The Bible says we are all born into sin. There was a situation in Phoenix recently where three young boys raped an eight-year-old girl. Where do you suppose they learned how to do that? When I was 10 or 11 years old, I would never have thought about something like that. They learned that behavior from the environment they lived in.

Do you think God is pleased with the nation today and the morals of the United States of America? I dare say that our founding fathers would be extremely displeased with what America has become, and they would say the moral fabric of America has been badly frayed and torn in our lifetimes. We have seen America go from a godly church going nation to one that is denying God altogether. There was a story on the news about a student who wanted his class to say the Pledge of Allegiance to the flag, and the school disallowed it because they were afraid someone might be offended. Since when is saying the Pledge of Allegiance offensive? The farther down the path this nation goes in denying God and worshiping other gods, the less we're going to see God's blessings on America.

GOD HAS A PLAN FOR YOUR LIFE

> *For I know the thoughts that I think toward you, says the Lord, thoughts of peace and not of evil, to give you a future and a hope. Then you will call upon Me and go and pray to Me, and I will listen to you. And you will seek Me and find Me, when you search for Me with all your heart.*
>
> Jeremiah 29:11–13 NKJV

This is one of the most powerful scriptures in the Bible.

God has a plan for you if you turn to him and listen to the Holy Spirit's voice. When you seek God with all of your heart, He says He will listen to you and give you a future full of hope. God knows what the future holds, and it is up to you to have the future He has planned for you or to go your own way. This scripture changed my life when I was going through a very rough time in my life. I happened to see it on a plaque in a store window and I started to pray this scripture and ask God take control of my future, and He did. My life was changed and I have followed His leading instead of trying to do everything on my own. He will give the peace you are looking for if you will listen to Him and seek Him with all of your heart.

GOD IS LIGHT

> *This is the message we have heard from him and declare to you: God is light; in him there is no darkness at all. If we claim to have fellowship with him and yet walk in the darkness, we lie and do not live out the truth. But if we walk in the light, as he is in the light, we have fellowship with one another, and the blood of Jesus, his Son, purifies us from all sin. If we claim to be without sin, we deceive ourselves and the truth is not in us. If we confess our sins, he is faithful and just and will forgive us our sins and purify us from all unrighteousness. If we claim we have not sinned, we make him out to be a liar and his word is not in us.*
>
> 1 John 1:5–10 NIV

Have you ever been in a really dark place; I mean pitch black, where you could see absolutely nothing? That's the way it feels when we are walking in sin. We are just feeling our way along and hoping we are going in the right direction. The problem with walking in the dark is you are not sure where you are going. You are in a black hole from which there is only one escape: **Jesus is the only way out of the darkness of sin.**

We can't stop sinning on our own and get out of that black hole. No matter how hard we try to be good and not sin, we can't do it without the light of Jesus.

But the way of the wicked is like deep darkness;
they do not know what makes them stumble.

Proverbs 4:19 NIV

We have all been there, stumbling around in the dark and not knowing what we fell over. Without the light of Jesus in our life we are going to stumble. It is inevitable. If we take our eyes off Christ and wander off on our own, we are going to fall every time.

If we claim to have fellowship with him and we don't, we lie and deceive ourselves.

There are a lot of people who claim to know Jesus and say they are Christians, but their lives don't reflect it. Living for Christ isn't just saying you are a Christian and that you intellectually believe He is the savior. A lot of people have head knowledge; they know who Jesus is and what he did, but their lives don't show others they are living a Godly example of how a Christian should live. There are a lot of people in churches today who show up on Sunday morning and listen to a sermon, but then they don't think about God the rest of the week. God doesn't want lip service; he doesn't want to be an afterthought in people's lives.

Only by living our lives in a way that reflects love and obedience to Christ will we truly have fellowship with him. **Being a Christian is a lifestyle: It is something you live and breathe every day of your life.**

GOD IS MY SALVATION

> *Surely God is my salvation, I will trust and not be afraid.*
> *The Lord, the Lord is my strength and my song;*
> *He has become my salvation.*
>
> Isaiah 12:2 NIV84

What a comforting thought: God is my salvation. He is always with you no matter what is going on in your life. I have heard said, "God abandoned me." No he didn't, you are the one who left, or maybe you haven't prayed and asked God for help. He will help you, but you have to ask Him first. God is a gentleman; He doesn't go where He is not wanted.

> *Never will I leave you;*
> *never will I forsake you.*
>
> Hebrews 13:5b NIV

Just because God doesn't answer right away, it doesn't mean he has abandoned you. God's timing is always perfect. He is always right on time: He is never too late or too early. He knows what the future holds and what it best for us. I look back on my life and can remember times when I should have listened to God and instead made a mess of things. But God is good and knows how to fix messes. He was there to put me back on the right path. Without Him guiding me I don't know where I would be, but with Him I know I am right where He wants me to be.

GOD IS OUR SHIELD AND PROTECTOR

David sang to the Lord the words of this song when the Lord delivered him from the hand of all his enemies and from the hand of Saul. He said:

> *The Lord is my rock, my fortress and my deliverer;*
> *my God is my rock, in whom I take refuge,*
> *my shield and the horn of my salvation.*
> *He is my stronghold, my refuge and my savior —*
> *from violent men you save me.*
> *I call to the Lord, who is worthy of praise,*
> *I am saved from my enemies.*
>
> 2 Samuel 22:1–5 NIV

David knew where his protection came from and he knew that it was the hand of God that kept from him being captured by Saul. Even great men like David are capable of falling into the hands of evil if they don't continually seek God's protection from temptation and the snares of Satan. The Bible tells us that David looked over and saw his neighbor Bathsheba bathing on her rooftop and he lusted in his heart. David had the option of walking back inside his house and closing the door. David had the option of asking God to forgive him for lusting after Bathsheba. David had been saved from a powerful enemy in King Saul and became the King of Israel, only to wind up falling into temptation as a result of his own failure to guard his heart and mind against evil.

DAVID MADE THE SAME MISTAKE MANY OF US DO.

David tried to rely on his own wisdom and his own intelligence to rationalize his way out of the sins he had committed. David slept with Bathsheba and thought that was the end of it. It was just between the two of them and what people do in the privacy of their own home is up to them. God has a way of reminding us of our sin. Bathsheba got pregnant and now David had a problem: Bathsheba was married. David granted Uriah leave, thinking he would sleep with his wife and people would think the baby was Uriah's. Uriah refused to sleep with her, feeling that he would be disrespecting his comrades, with them sleeping on the cold hard ground and he with his wife. David would have avoided all of that if he would have just prayed what Jabez did: "Keep me from Evil, so that I will be free from pain."

GOD IS OUR SHIELD AND OUR PROTECTOR, BUT ONLY WHEN WE STAY BEHIND HIM AND LET HIM PROTECT US.

GOD WILL PROVIDE

> *I have received full payment and have more than enough. I am amply supplied, now that I have received from Epaphroditus the gifts you sent. They are a fragrant offering, an acceptable sacrifice pleasing to God. And my God will meet all your needs according to the riches of his glory in Christ. To our God and father be the glory forever and ever. Amen.*
>
> Philippians 4:18–19 NIV

Paul was relying on God to meet all of his needs, and he thanked God when people gave him food, shelter and clothing to meet his needs and the needs of his ministry. You will have everything you want and need. While it is true we all need to work to make a living, as a society we have become so dependent on ourselves and pride ourselves on being independent to the point that we leave God out of the equation. Men say, work hard and obey the God of the almighty dollar, and we tend to forget to ask God what we are supposed to do for a living and how we are to spend the money we get. Godly wisdom is more precious than all the money in the world if we seek him first.

GOD'S EVERLASTING LOVE

As far as the east is from the west,
So far has he removed our transgressions from us.
As a father has compassion on his children,
so the Lord has compassion on those who fear him;
for he knows how we are formed,
he remembers that we are dust.
The life of mortals is like grass,
they flourish like a flower of the field;
the wind blows over it and it is gone,
and its place remembers it no more.
But from everlasting to everlasting
the Lord's love is with those who fear him,
and his righteousness with their children's children—
with those who keep his covenant
and remember to obey his precepts.

Psalm 103:12–18 NIV

God's love and compassion know no limits and He promises to be with us all the days of our lives, if we will trust and obey the precepts He has laid out for us in His Word. Your sins are forgiven and forgotten; every day is a brand-new day to show your love for Him, as He does for us. The love that God has for us is impossible for us to understand, because God is omnipresent. He is everywhere, He knows everything, and He knows what the future holds. If we knew everything God knows. we would not be able to handle it. God purposely gave us a limited capacity for understanding things, so He could take care of us; and—even if make horrible mistakes—He is willing to forgive us. His grace covers our sins and we can keep moving forward, knowing God is going to be with us all the way.

GOD'S GIFT OF GRACE

> *For I am the least of the apostles and do not even deserve to be called an apostle, because I persecuted the church of God. But by the grace of God I am what I am, and his grace to me was not without effect. No, I worked harder than all of them—yet not I, but the grace of God that was with me. Whether, then, it is I or they, this is what we preach, and this is what you believed.*
>
> 1 Corinthians 15:9–11 NIV

Paul knew where He came from. He knew he didn't not deserve God's grace upon his life. He worked very hard for the cause of Christ and the salvation of souls.

GOOD SALT

> *You are the salt of the earth. But if the salt loses its saltiness, how can it be made salty again? It is no longer good for anything, except to be thrown out and trampled by men.*
>
> Matthew 5:13 NIV

To refer to someone as the salt of the earth is a high compliment. It means that person is very well respected and has a great deal of integrity. The kind of person who would go out of his way to help someone in need. Someone you would be proud to call your friend; someone who is pure in heart and motive.

Salt in the Ancient World was a symbol of purity. It was used to preserve and to purify food. Before there were such things as refrigeration and ice readily available, people used salt to preserve meat. People would kill an animal, dry the meat, and then cure it with salt. If you have ever had beef jerky, you probably noticed it is very salty. If Christians are to be the salt of the earth, we must be examples of purity. We must be the ones who set the standard for others to follow. Sticking to standards of honesty by not cutting corners but doing what is right. Not lying to cover up a mistake; being willing to admit our own shortcomings. Being conscientious in everything we do and doing it to the best of our ability. Even if you don't like your job and maybe despise your boss, it is still your responsibility to do the best you can and put in an honest day's work for a day's pay. If we are to be the salt of the earth, we need to be honest in everything we do. We need to set the moral standards in our conduct and in our speech. We can't be the salt of the earth if we are telling off-color jokes and laughing at those kinds of jokes. Or reading books that contain a lot of sex and violence in them. We can't sit around and drink with our friends on the one hand and be telling them about Jesus on the other. We can't withdraw from the world and become hermits, but we can't be influenced by the world either.

> *If anyone considers himself religious and yet does not keep a tight rein on his tongue, he deceives himself and his religion is worthless. Religion that God our Father accepts as pure and faultless is this: to look after orphans and widows in their distress and to keep oneself from being polluted by the world.*
>
> James 1:26–27 NIV 84

Have you ever been around meat that has gone bad? People that are not pure in heart are a stench in God's nostrils. We are to be the salt that preserves this world from corruption; we are the preservers of the right standards of conduct, morality, and honesty. We should be making it easier for those around us to be good. If people know you are a Christian, they are usually more careful about what they say and do around you.

Many years ago, when I was still in the Army, I was having a bad day and was very frustrated. People I worked with knew I was a Christian and that I kept a small New Testament on my desk.

This particular day I was very frustrated, and I uttered a swear word right at the time my boss walked in the office. He looked at me and laughed and said, " I can't believe you said that."

Then he yelled out, "Hey guys, guess what Young just said!" laughing the whole time.

I immediately felt humiliated and ashamed because I let my Savior down. I learned a very valuable lesson that day about being careful what I said and did, because people *do* watch what you do and say. Being the salt of the earth means always being aware of your actions and setting the example for others around you.

GREAT IS THE LORD

> Sing to the Lord, all the earth;
> proclaim his salvation day after day.
> Declare his glory among the nations,
> his marvelous deeds among all peoples.
> For great is the Lord and most worthy of praise;
> he is to be feared above all gods.
> For all the gods of the nations are idols,
> but the Lord made the heavens.
> Splendor and majesty are before him;
> strength and joy are in his dwelling place.
>
> 1 Chronicles 16:23–27 NIV

If you just look around you the glory of God is everywhere.

He is the only God who made the heavens and the earth.

He is the only God who can bring salvation to your soul and peace to your life.

No matter what your circumstances are right now, He is there with you and He understands. Praise Him now: Great is the Lord and most worthy of Praise!

GREATER IS HE

> *To this John replied, "A man can receive only what is given him from heaven. You yourselves can testify that I said, 'I am not the Christ but am sent ahead of him.' The bride belongs to the bridegroom. The friend who attends the bridegroom waits and listens for him, and is full of joy when he hears the bridegroom's voice. That joy is mine, and it is now complete. He must become greater; I must become less. The one who comes from above is above all; the one who is from the earth belongs to the earth, and speaks as one from the earth. The one who comes from heaven is above all."*
>
> John 3:27–31 NIV

John knew what his place was in Christ's ministry. He knew that it wasn't about him but about Jesus. He knew that he had to become less in order for Christ to become more in his life. We have a tendency to forget that and try to take more on ourselves than we should. Christians get frustrated and angry when they don't see results in someone else's life. That is because we are trying to minister to people based on our thinking and our opinions and not on what the Holy Spirit wants us to do. We should always be very careful telling someone what Christ will and will not do in their lives. We should always make sure that people know that whatever happens has to be God's will. We cannot do anything on our own. We can't heal anyone, we can't save anyone, we can't do anything. Only Jesus Christ can do those things, and it is by being in tune with the Holy Spirit that we can know what His will is. I have heard people tell someone this is God's will for your life! Oh really! Since when can you speak for God? We can pray that God's will be done, and we can encourage people to seek God about whatever the situation is, but we cannot absolutely say that God is going to do a particular thing in someone's life. Whenever we pray for someone to be healed, we are asking God to heal them and believing that they will be healed. We cannot absolutely say that person will be healed, because a large part of that equation is faith. It is only by yielding ourselves completely to Christ that our faith will grow. As long as you are depending on your own resources, your faith will not grow. John the Baptist knew that the power of his ministry came from God and that is why he humbled himself to the point of living in the desert, wearing animal skins, and eating locusts and wild honey. John became nothing so that Christ could become everything in his life. He knew that his whole purpose in being born was to be the one to introduce Jesus to the world. That is something that a lot of people don't understand: You were born to serve and to please God.

And we know that in all things God works for the good of those who love him,
who have been called according to his purpose.

Romans 8:28 NIV

In order to find Him, we have to humble ourselves before Him. We must become lesser so that He can become greater in our lives. We get so busy trying to figure out what God's will is in our lives that we forget to stop and seek Him. We shouldn't have to figure it out; it should be clear. When someone says I believe this is God's will for my life, they had better have spent much time in prayer and seeking God. Just because it seems like a good idea, doesn't necessarily mean it is God's will.

If you have something on your mind and are not sure what to do, take it to the Lord and ask Him what His will is concerning this matter. Once He shows you what His will is, you will have your answer. Remember, everything we do should honor and glorify Him above our own will.

HAPPY AS YOU ARE

> *But godliness with contentment is great gain. For we brought nothing into the world, and we can take nothing out of it. But if we have food and clothing, we will be content with that. Those who want to get rich fall into temptation and a trap into many foolish and harmful desires that plunge people into ruin and destruction. For the love of money is a root of all kinds of evil. Some people, eager for money, have wandered from the faith and pierced themselves with many griefs.*
>
> 1 Timothy 6:6–10 NIV

Happiness seems to be a moving target for a lot of people. They are constantly looking for what will make them happy and, when they find what they are looking for, they find it doesn't give them the happiness they thought it would. They finally get so despondent because they can't find the one thing that will make them happy, they take their own lives.

So far in 2022 there have been 1419 suicides in the State of Arizona—and Arizona isn't even in the top ten states that have the highest suicide rate. The only thing that will bring true happiness is a relationship with Jesus Christ. He is the only one who can give you true happiness and peace that will calm your soul and make you content in Him. Every year we hear about celebrities who take their own lives because they are depressed and unhappy. They have everything this world can offer them. But they don't have Jesus in their lives.

Finding happiness is really very simple: All you have to do is put your faith and trust in Jesus Christ. Nothing in this world can give you what Jesus can. Sadly, some people never call upon the name of Jesus and live miserable lives in spite of all they have in material things.

Know Jesus, Know Peace. No Jesus, No Peace.

I pray that each of you find peace and happiness by calling upon Jesus Christ, the Prince of Peace.

HAVE NO FEAR

Fear is something that we all experience sometime in our life. Sometimes it is very real and we call out for help, hoping there is someone around to help. The first thing most people do is call out to God—even if they have never talked to God.

> *But now, thus says the Lord, who created you, O Jacob,*
> *And He who formed you, O Israel:*
> *"Fear not, for I have redeemed you;*
> *I have called you by your name;*
> *You are Mine.*
> *When you pass through the waters, I will be with you;*
> *And through the rivers, they shall not overflow you.*
> *When you walk through the fire, you shall not be burned,*
> *nor shall the flame scorch you.*
> *For I am the Lord your God,*
> *The Holy One of Israel, your Savior."*
>
> Isaiah 43:1–3a NKJV

The Prophet Isaiah was trying to get the children of Israel to understand that, no matter what happened, God would be with them. Even fires and floods would not harm them. But the caveat was they had to be obedient and listen to what God was telling them to do. Sometimes we think we know what is best and are able to figure out what is best for us on our own.

I have heard of people who, when their neighborhood was on fire or being flooded out, decided to stay with their homes rather than evacuate. Some of those people died for their earthly possessions. When a boat comes by to get you and you tell them to go on without you, did you ever think maybe God sent that boat to save you? There is a difference between being brave and being stupid. Listening to God is the smartest thing you can do. He will be with you no matter what happens. Nobody knows what the future is going to hold for any of us. The Bible tells us many, many times not to be afraid. Have enough faith to take Him at his word.

HE CRIED FOR YOU

> *As he approached Jerusalem and saw the city, he wept over it and said, "If you, even you, had only known on this day what would bring you peace—but now it is hidden from your eyes. The days will come upon you when your enemies will build an embankment against you and encircle you and hem you in on every side. They will dash you to the ground, you and the children within your walls. They will not leave one stone on another, because you did not recognize the time of God's coming to you.*
>
> Luke 19:41–44 NIV

Christ's triumphal entry into Jerusalem was a time of great joy and also a time of great sorrow. People were yelling and praising God as He was about to enter the city. But Jesus was crying! Why would He be crying and be sorrowful about the best day He would have here on earth? It wasn't because He knew his time on earth was nearing the end. It was because He knew these same people who were cheering Him would betray Him and that Jerusalem would eventually be destroyed for its sinful behavior. Judas Iscariot was the most famous person who would betray Him, but the truth is, by the time the week was over, everyone there that day would betray Him. Not one soul would come to Jesus' defense and acknowledge Him as the Son of God. Jesus was weeping not only for Jerusalem, but for everyone who would reject Him in the future. It is not His will that anyone should perish—John 3:16 tells us that. The reason people turned against Jesus was because they loved darkness instead of light. As soon as they realized that Jesus wasn't the earthly king they were looking for, one who was going to overthrow the Roman government and bring them peace and prosperity here on earth, they turned against Him even though they knew that the scriptures foretold His coming. They couldn't see beyond their own selfish desires and what their idea was of a messiah. About seven hundred years before, the prophet Isaiah gave a very clear picture of what the messiah was going to be like. There were very clear signs to look for. They wanted things to change, but only in a way that would benefit them, not in a way that would reap eternal benefits they could not even imagine.

He cried for you and a week later He died for you. But then came Sunday Morning and He rose triumphantly from the grave and conquered sin and death for you. Remember when He was on the cross, you were on his mind. HE HAS RISEN!

HE IS THE POTTER, WE ARE THE CLAY

Yet you, Lord, are our Father.
We are the clay, you are the potter;
we are all the work of your hand.
Do not be angry beyond measure, Lord;
do not remember our sins forever.
Oh, look on us, we pray,
for we are all your people

Isaiah 64:8–9 NIV

We are God's creation, designed by Him, for Him; in order to serve Him. If we allow our creator to shape us and form us into what He would have us to be, we would be much happier. Unfortunately, when we allow sin to enter our lives, we become something that our creator never intended. It is only when we allow Him to take charge of our lives that we find our true purpose and the reason we are living. Let your creator shape you in His image today.

HE IS THE VINE AND WE ARE THE BRANCHES

I am the true vine, and my Father is the gardener. He cuts off every branch in me that bears no fruit, while every branch that does bear fruit he prunes so that it will be even more fruitful. You are already clean because of the word I have spoken to you. Remain in me, as I also remain in you. No branch can bear fruit by itself; it must remain in the vine. Neither can you bear fruit unless you remain in me. I am the vine; you are the branches. If you remain in me and I in you, you will bear much fruit; apart from me you can do nothing. If you do not remain in me, you are like a branch that is thrown away and withers; such branches are picked up, thrown into the fire and burned. If you remain in me and my words remain in you, ask whatever you wish, and it will be done for you. This is to my Father's glory, that you bear much fruit, showing yourselves to be my disciples. As the Father has loved me, so have I loved you. Now remain in my love. If you keep my commands, you will remain in my love, just as I have kept my Father's commands and remain in his love. I have told you this so that my joy may be in you and that your joy may be complete. My command is this: Love each other as I have loved you.

John 15:1–12 NIV

Jesus gives a vivid illustration of how we are to live our lives. If we are not being fruitful, we are of no use to the kingdom of God. Anybody who knows anything about gardening knows that you have to prune the dead branches away or the dead branches will take the strength away from the living ones. Typically, with most fruit trees, if you prune the tree way back in the fall, it will give you better fruit in the spring. Our lives reflect the kind of fruit that we will bear. It is so important to prune all of the junk out of our lives that distract us from concentrating on our Christian walk. Our commitment to him on a daily basis through prayer and spending time reading the bible is the best way to continue to grow in our walk with the Lord. Just as a tree or a vine needs water and nutrients to grow, so do our souls. We can't grow apart from God. Renewing our commitment to Christ daily is the best way to do that. It's tough to live a focused life. From every direction something or someone clamors for our attention. We get distracted and the next thing we know we are off in a different direction from where we intended to go and wind up going off to a place where we never intended to go.

Bearing fruit is more than just winning souls for Christ; It is how we live our lives.

Be joyful always, pray continually, give thanks in all circumstances, for this is God's will for you in Christ Jesus.

1 Thessalonians 5:16–18 NIV

You can pray anywhere and at anytime. God wants us to keep the lines of communication open. If you ask anything in His name, it shall be done. **We are to be joyful and give thanks in all circumstances.** It is easy to be joyful when life is good, and things are going well. It is a different story when our lives have been turned upside down. True joy comes from having a consistent relationship with Him and knowing that He will help us through the tough times and be there with us. Being joyful doesn't mean we are supposed to be happy all the time. There is a difference between being happy and being joyful. It means having that inner joy of knowing His Holy Spirit is living and dwelling in us, and that we have Jesus to lean on, even when we don't feel like praying and praising Him. We know that He is there: He said He would never leave us or forsake us. We are to love each other as Jesus loved us. That is why going to church and having that fellowship with other believers is so important. Someone said no man is an island, we all need help, encouragement, love, and reassurance. Jesus loved the unlovable and He loved us enough to die for us. The fruit Jesus was talking about is this:

> But the fruit of the Spirit is love, joy, peace, longsuffering, kindness, goodness, faithfulness, gentleness, self-control. Against such there is no law. And those who are Christ's have crucified the flesh with its passions and desires. If we live in the Spirit, let us also walk in the Spirit. Let us not become conceited, provoking one another, envying one another.
>
> Galatians 5:22–26 NKJV

We should do our best every day to bear fruit that leads people to a relationship with Jesus Christ. It is very important that what we say and do glorifies our Savior; you never know when someone is watching your life and through you, they may come to Christ.

HEARING AND BELIEVING

> *Most assuredly, I say to you, he who hears My word and believes in Him who sent Me has everlasting life, and shall not come into judgment, but has passed from death into life. Most assuredly, I say to you, the hour is coming, and now is, when the dead will hear the voice of the Son of God; and those who hear will live.*
>
> John 5:24–25 NKJV

The scripture is very clear that Christ will return and will take those that have believed and accepted Jesus Christ as their savior home to heaven with him. Those that know Jesus as their savior will not face judgment, because their sins have been forgiven and they are children of God, living with Him in heaven forever. What a wonderful thing to look forward to, knowing you have a home in heaven and a new life when this one is over. There will be no more death or pain or sorrow—only rejoicing in heaven with others who have gone before you.

HEARING VOICES IN YOUR HEAD

The boy Samuel ministered before the LORD under Eli. In those days the word of the LORD was rare; there were not many visions. One night Eli, whose eyes were becoming so weak that he could barely see, was lying down in his usual place. The lamp of God had not yet gone out, and Samuel was lying down in the temple of the LORD, where the ark of God was. Then the LORD called Samuel. Samuel answered, "Here I am." And he ran to Eli and said, "Here I am; you called me." But Eli said, "I did not call; go back and lie down." So he went and lay down. Again the LORD called, "Samuel!" And Samuel got up and went to Eli and said, "Here I am; you called me." "My son," Eli said, "I did not call; go back and lie down." Now Samuel did not yet know the LORD: The word of the LORD had not yet been revealed to him. The LORD called Samuel a third time, and Samuel got up and went to Eli and said, "Here I am; you called me." Then Eli realized that the LORD was calling the boy. So Eli told Samuel, "Go and lie down, and if he calls you, say, 'Speak, LORD, for your servant is listening.'" So Samuel went and lay down in his place. The LORD came and stood there, calling as at the other times, "Samuel! Samuel!" Then Samuel said, "Speak, for your servant is listening."

1 Samuel 3:1-10 NIV84

Have you ever had an overwhelming feeling God was speaking to you?

Have you ever wondered if it is really God or your imagination?

Listening and responding to God is vital in a relationship with God.

God doesn't always speak in an audible voice; He does speak to us clearly through His word. To receive His message, we must be ready to listen and act upon what He tells us and say "Here I am Lord, your servant is listening." Sometimes I tend to be suspicious when people say that God told them to do something. After all, hearing from God, or saying you have, is a very serious matter. People for centuries talked about this overwhelming feeling that God was speaking to them. It is not something that necessarily comes naturally to us; we have to listen for that still, small voice. Sometimes that voice may be convicting us of sin, assuring us of God's love or telling us to do something.

According to a survey in Newsweek magazine, more Americans said they pray in a given week than work, exercise, or have sexual relations. Of the 13 percent of Americans who claim to be agnostic or atheist, one in five prays daily. So why are we so ambivalent about God talking to us? Lily Tomlin spoke these lines in the play *The Search for Signs of Intelligent Life in the Universe:* "Why is it that when we speak to God we are said to be praying, but when God speaks to us we are said to be schizophrenic?" If we can speak to God, what is so odd about God speaking to us? Being open and receptive to the leading of the Holy Spirit is a requirement for living a Spirit-lead life. People today are expectantly waiting for a mighty outpouring of the Holy Spirit upon the earth. It has happened before—it can happen again. But it won't happen until people begin to experience a deeper knowledge and relationship with God. Until people are really sensitive to leading of the Holy Spirit in their lives, they can't experience the presence of God the way people did in the Bible. You don't need to be a pastor or a spiritual leader in order to hear from God in profound way. God spoke through ordinary people—even sinful and deceitful people—in the Bible.

All you have to do is listen for that still small voice and, if it is God, He will never lead you in the wrong direction. His way is always the best way.

HEAVENLY BODIES

> *"Death is swallowed up in victory. O Death, where is your sting? O Hades, where is your victory?" The sting of death is sin, and the strength of sin is the law. But thanks be to God, who gives us the victory through our Lord Jesus Christ.*
>
> 1 Corinthians 15:54–57 NKJV

There is a saying that goes, "Don't complain about getting older, there are many who never got the chance."

That is what Memorial Day is all about, remembering those who never came home while fighting for this nation. There are many who did come home who suffer from PTSD and their lives are not the same because of the horrors they saw and the things they had to do while in combat. I am thankful that I never was in combat and didn't see the things that many did.

I am thankful for every day that the Lord gives me. I am looking forward to the day that the promise given in 1 Corinthians 15 will come true in my life, and I will put on a brand new heavenly body that won't get old and sick, but will last forever. Those that died for our country went from the horrors of war to the arms of Jesus.

We should always remember the great sacrifice that was given by many so you can enjoy the freedoms you have in the United States of America. God bless the USA.

HEZEKIAH'S HEALING AND GOD'S WILL

In those days Hezekiah became ill and was at the point of death. The prophet Isaiah son of Amoz went to him and said, "This is what the Lord says: Put your house in order, because you are going to die; you will not recover."

Hezekiah turned his face to the wall and prayed to the Lord, "Remember, Lord, how I have walked before you faithfully and with wholehearted devotion and have done what is good in your eyes." And Hezekiah wept bitterly.

Before Isaiah had left the middle court, the word of the Lord came to him: "Go back and tell Hezekiah, the ruler of my people, 'This is what the Lord, the God of your father David, says: I have heard your prayer and seen your tears; I will heal you. On the third day from now you will go up to the temple of the Lord. I will add fifteen years to your life. And I will deliver you and this city from the hand of the king of Assyria. I will defend this city for my sake and for the sake of my servant David.'"

Then Isaiah said, "Prepare a poultice of figs." They did so and applied it to the boil, and he recovered.

Hezekiah had asked Isaiah, "What will be the sign that the Lord will heal me and that I will go up to the temple of the Lord on the third day from now?"

Isaiah answered, "This is the Lord's sign to you that the Lord will do what he has promised: Shall the shadow go forward ten steps, or shall it go back ten steps?"

"It is a simple matter for the shadow to go forward ten steps," said Hezekiah. "Rather, have it go back ten steps."

Then the prophet Isaiah called on the Lord, and the Lord made the shadow go back the ten steps it had gone down on the stairway of Ahaz.

2 Kings 20:1–11 NIV

In an earlier devotion I talked about how healing has to glorify God and be His will. Hezekiah's healing did just that. The Lord told Hezekiah that He would heal him and he would live fifteen more years and, as proof of this, He set the sundial back ten steps. The sundial's shadow, which measured the time, was moved back by the Lord as part of his promise to Hezekiah. The Lord healed Hezekiah as part of a promise to defeat Assyria, their enemy. Hezekiah had done God's will up to a point. A group of foreign dignitaries came to visit and Hezekiah showed them everything in the Kingdom, including all the gold in his vault. This angered God because the king had showed everything in the kingdom to people who would become his enemies. God told Hezekiah that Judah would be defeated by Babylon and all the people would become slaves in captivity. He promised Hezekiah this would not happen until after his death.

Hezekiah's healing and the sun being set back showed off God's power and His Glory. This story tells us that everything in the world is controlled by God, even life and death. We have to live our lives in obedience to God's will and He will take care of us.

Each of us is alive to serve God and to fulfill a purpose He has for us. In order to find out our purpose, we have to accept Jesus Christ as our Savior and the Holy Spirit will reveal to us our purpose. It is never too late to start living God's purpose for your life. One way or another His purpose is always fulfilled. When you start working to fulfill God's will in your life, you will have a sense of peace and joy that is wonderful, something you have never experienced before.

HOPE IN CHRIST

There is a place called hope and Jesus Christ lives there.

In order to get there all you have to do is invite him in to your life.

> Here I am! I stand at the door and knock. If anyone hears my voice and
> opens the door, I will come in and eat with that person, and they with me.
>
> Revelation 3:20 NIV

None of us know what the future holds, but he said he would supply our needs according to his riches in glory.

If it is sickness, he said his grace is sufficient.

If it is death, we have a home with him waiting for us in heaven.

No matter what trials we face, he said he would never leave us or forsake us. All we have to do is put our faith and trust in him.

Who or what are you putting your trust in?

Put your trust in the one who never breaks his promises, his name is Jesus Christ

HOPE THROUGH CHRIST

> *Therefore, since we have been justified through faith, we have peace with God through our Lord Jesus Christ, through whom we have gained access by faith into this grace in which we now stand. And we rejoice in the hope of the glory of God. Not only so, but we also rejoice in our sufferings, because we know that suffering produces perseverance; perseverance, character; and character, hope. And hope does not disappoint us, because God has poured out his love into our hearts by the Holy Spirit, whom he has given us.*
> Romans 5:1–6 NIV84

Hope can be a very elusive thing, one that is very hard to turn into reality. Every year people make New Years resolutions, where they hope that they can attain some elusive goal. They start out really motivated and, for the first week or so, things go really well. Then reality sets in and life gets in the way. Those good intentions fall by the wayside, and they fall back into their old habits. That's because, in order to reach any kind of a goal, you have to have a great amount of discipline and be willing to work hard and do what it takes to achieve the goal that you have set for yourself.

THE ONLY REAL HOPE AND THE ONLY REAL GOAL THAT WILL BE LONG

LASTING IS OUR HOPE IN JESUS CHRIST.

That also takes work, but the difference is that we have the Holy Spirit to help us along and motivate us to continue towards the goal of doing God's will in our lives and eventually eternal life in heaven with Him. Paul said that we rejoice in our suffering because suffering produces perseverance. We all know that suffering is a part of life, and we don't always understand why we suffer the things that we do. What we do know is Christ said He would be there for us. Jesus Christ is real and placing your faith and hope in Him is something you can count on. He will always be there for you no matter what happens in your life.

HOW TO LIVE A HOLY LIFE

What does it mean to live a holy life? According to Webster, holiness is the quality or state of being holy. How do we do that? Is it possible to live a holy life, and still be human?

Holiness seeks to be like God. When you accept Jesus Christ as your savior, you receive His holiness and His Holy Spirit, by His grace. This is not a one time transaction; it is a daily, moment by moment striving to live more by the spirit and less by the flesh.

A while ago, a friend of mine bought his daughter a car. It had to sit in the garage until her sixteenth birthday. Holiness is like a gift already purchased for us by the blood of Christ. But we cannot have full use of it until a certain date in the future, when we will go to heaven and be glorified in Christ.

> *I beseech you therefore, brethren, by the mercies of God, that you present your bodies a living sacrifice, holy, acceptable to God, which is your reasonable service. And do not be conformed to this world, but be transformed by the renewing of your mind, that you may prove what is that good and acceptable and perfect will of God.*
>
> Romans 12:1–2 NKJV

Holiness is a process which includes God's part and our part. Whenever you put yourself under a doctors care, he can't help you if you don't follow his instructions. Many times, as the patient surrenders his own ideas, he becomes well. If we want to be made holy, we must willingly surrender ourselves to the Lord's care and actively obey His instructions. We have no more power to make ourselves Holy than a dying man has to save himself. We are weak and tired and can't offer much help. However, we can submit to His rehab program. The key to our part is faith. To seek Him in obedience. True religion must have substance, integrity and purity; these are the thought and emotional patterns engraved on our minds. These internal habit patterns play just as forceful a role as external influences on our actions. In fact perhaps even more so since, as unbelievers, we formerly gave ourselves up to developing habits of unholiness. Some of these habits are hard to break on our own. It is only by prayer, faith, and a lot of hard work on our part that we can break whatever is holding us back.

HUMILITY VS PRIDE

> *God opposes the proud but gives grace to the humble. Submit yourselves, then, to God.*
> *Resist the devil, and he will flee from you. Come near to God and he will come near to*
> *you. Wash your hands, you sinners, and purify your hearts, you double-minded. Grieve,*
> *mourn and wail. Change your laughter to mourning and your joy to gloom. Humble*
> *yourselves before the Lord, and he will lift you up.*
>
> James 4:6–11 NIV84

People who fail are so full of pride. They think they can't fail, and that asking for help is a sign of weakness. People who cheat other people out of their homes and their life savings have no remorse because they are not capable of seeing what they did was wrong. Money has become their God and when they do fail, they are left with nothing.

There are people today who are running this country that are only out for themselves. They don't care about rising gas prices and higher interest rates because it doesn't affect them.

Our only hope is to humble ourselves before God and ask for his protection. God will never fail us. Politicians come and go but God is always with us. My prayer is that this time of price increases will pass, but there is coming a time when it won't pass. People are going to be starving and relying on the government for everything. That is exactly what they want. They have already tried to shut down the churches with COVID and they are not going to stop trying unless God's people stand up and fight for our God given right to gather together without fear of retribution. God is an ever-present help in time of trouble and we need to live like we believe that and not cower in fear at Satan's tactics.

HURRIED TO DEATH

> *I beseech you therefore, brethren, by the mercies of God, that you present your bodies a living sacrifice, holy, acceptable to God, which is your reasonable service. And do not be conformed to this world, but be transformed by the renewing of your mind, that you may prove what is that good and acceptable and perfect will of God.*
>
> Romans 12:1–2 NKJV

HURRY SICKNESS: A malaise where a person feels chronically short of time, and so tends to perform every task faster, and gets flustered when encountering any kind of delay.

Time magazine noted that, back in the 1960s, expert testimony was given to a subcommittee of the Senate on time management. The essence of it was that, because of advances in technology, within twenty years or so, people would have to radically cut back on how many hours a week they worked, or how many weeks a year they worked, or else they would have to start retiring sooner. The great challenge, they said, was what people would do with all their free time. Yet fifty years later, not many of us would say that our primary challenge in regard to time is what to do with all the excess.

We will buy anything that promises to help us hurry. The best-selling shampoo in America rose to the top because it combines shampoo and conditioner in one step, eliminating the need for the second step, and eliminating the time people have spend using a rinse on their hair. Dominos became the number one name in pizza because they promised to deliver in thirty minutes or less. Their CEO said, "We don't sell pizza, we sell delivery." A Detroit hospital guarantees that emergency room patients will be seen within 20 minutes or treatment is free. We worship at the shrine of the Golden Arches, not because they sell good food or even cheap food, but because it is fast food.

Yet, in spite of all these things and thousands more that are supposed to save us time and make our lives easier, we are still hurrying everywhere and don't have enough time in a day to get everything done that we need to accomplish.

People are having heart attacks every day and dying because of stress. When Sunday comes around, they are too busy or too tired to go to church. Romans 12:2 says to make our bodies a living sacrifice to God by renewing our minds. That means to change our thinking and to spend more time reading our Bible and praying. I used to be one of those people that were on the go 12 hours a day, 7 days a week. It took getting very sick and having to retire because of stress for God to get my attention—God will get your attention one way or another. I realized that I wasn't spending time in His word and praying. I was trying to handle everything on my own and failed miserably. That is when I rededicated my life to God, asking him to help me by guiding me and helping me make the right decisions. It doesn't matter how much money you make or what position you hold, if you don't have God in your life, you are a miserable failure, because God isn't interested in what you have or who you are: On Judgment Day, he will want to know what you have done for him. That is all that matters; nothing else matters and it isn't worth losing your soul over. If this is what you are experiencing, give it all to God and let him renew your mind and your soul.

INHERITANCE

> *Lord, you alone are my inheritance, my cup of blessing.*
> *You guard all that is mine.*
>
> Psalm 16:5 NLT

It is very nice when a parent is able to leave an inheritance of some kind to their children in the form of money or some other item that they consider valuable.

Those things are only temporary and will not last forever.

The only thing we can leave behind for our children that *is* forever is the saving knowledge of Jesus Christ. Make sure our children know who Jesus Christ is and that His saving grace will insure their place in heaven—where the real riches are waiting for everyone who knows Jesus as their Lord and Savior. We cannot save our children, but we can make sure they know who can and will if they will ask.

Start children off on the way they should go,
and even when they are old they will not turn from it

Proverbs 22:6 NIV

Raising children in the church and seeing them turn away from God is heartbreaking. This scripture tells us to do our part and let the Lord do the rest. I have talked to many people who were raised in church and for a while went their own way. As they got older, they realized they needed God in their life. Never give up on your children. This scripture promises that the Holy Spirit will continue to gently remind them of their upbringing. You may not see it in your lifetime, but God doesn't want to see anyone lost.

That is the best inheritance you can leave them.

IS MARRIAGE STILL RELEVANT IN TODAY'S SOCIETY?

Marriage isn't just a bunch of words you say in front of a minister; they are a solemn vow before God. If I were to take a poll, many of you would say you know a couple who are living together without being married. Many people feel that marriage is no longer relevant and is outdated, so there is no reason to get married.

> *You shall not commit adultery*
>
> Exodus 20:14

That is one of the ten commandments. If you are living together and having sex without being married, you are committing adultery.

There are many passages in the Bible that talk about marriage and divorce which I won't list here. In marriage you will love and cherish each other the rest of your lives. That can be a very long time, and a lot of things happen that people never expect. I don't believe that anyone gets married planning to get a divorce if things don't work out.

I have found the main reason marriages fail is a lack of communication. It is very important that couples talk to each other and do things together. Most people spend more time with their coworkers than they do their spouse. Work is important. After all, you have to make money in order to live. But the vow you made before God to your spouse is more important. Making time for your spouse is the most important thing you can do. Whenever you were dating you were inseparable. What happened? Life happened, you started a family, you started spending more time at work. Marriage is a commitment like no other you will ever make, and it takes more work than your job to have a happy marriage. Marriage is very important because children need two parents living together and working together to raise those children in a Christ-based home.

Divorce should be a last resort, not something you do the first time life starts getting hard and you have a big argument. I know of what I speak: before I recommitted my life to Christ, I was divorced and it was one of the worst times in my life. Then I vowed to live my life for Christ and God forgave me for getting divorced. Divorce isn't the unpardonable sin, but couples should do their best to save their marriage before they talk about divorce. Today I am happily married and my wife and I, before we got married, promised each other to commit our marriage to Christ and we have. Every marriage should include a man, a woman and Christ.

There was a book written called "Every Man's Battle" by Stephen Arterburn that talks about sexual temptation. Every man is tempted to commit adultery at some point. It is a very hard battle that men have to ask God to help them fight—and win.

I the Lord do not change.

Malachi 3:6

God's word is the same yesterday, today and tomorrow. God doesn't change and neither does his commands that he gave us on how to live our lives. Marriage is as relevant today as it was thousands of years ago. If you commit your marriage and each other to Christ, your marriage will be happy and never fail.

IS THE BIRTH OF CHRIST STILL RELEVANT IN TODAY'S CULTURE?

Christmas is the most wonderful holiday of the year, but yet it is amazing how many people miss the point of why we celebrate Christmas. Just as there was no room in the Inn for him on that night so many years ago, people don't have room for him in their hearts today. Jesus is shoved aside to some place out of sight and out of mind.

> *Suddenly a great company of the heavenly host appeared with the angel, praising God and saying, "Glory to God in the highest and on earth peace to men on whom his favor rests." When the angels had left them and gone into heaven, the shepherds said to one another, "Let's go to Bethlehem and see this thing that has happened, which the Lord has told us about." So they hurried off and found Mary and Joseph, and the baby, who was lying in the manger. When they had seen him, they spread the word concerning what had been told them about this child, and all who heard it were amazed at what the shepherds said to them. But Mary treasured up all these things and pondered them in her heart. The shepherds returned, glorifying and praising God for all the things they had heard and seen which were just as they had been told.*
>
> Luke 2:13-20 NIV

Jesus is shoved aside to some place out of sight and out of mind. People have been trying to refute the birth of Christ for 2000 years. There were similar stories in ancient lore about the virgin birth of a child, but those stories have been long forgotten, except by those trying to disprove the facts of Christ's birth. The fact that His birth has had such a profound effect on the world for so many years gives credence to the fact that it is true. Even Herod the king believed it was true and tried to have baby Jesus killed. People are trying to kill Jesus by removing nativity scenes and the name of God from public buildings. But you can't kill that which is eternal. God is from everlasting to everlasting; no matter how hard they try, the name of Christ will never be completely obliterated from society. They can't remove that which is living and dwelling inside of every Christian in the world today.

Another amazing part of this story is that the angels appeared to the shepherds in the field. The shepherds were the outcasts of society, they were dirty and smelled bad, since they lived with the sheep in the fields for most of the time. They were considered unclean and were not allowed in the temple, so there is very little chance they were even aware of the scriptures concerning the birth of the Messiah. God in his wisdom let the poor and the outcast of society know about Christ's birth before anyone else. The greatest sermon ever preached was delivered that night to a group of frightened shepherds, who were told not to be afraid, but to rejoice because their Savior had been born in Bethlehem.

The world during that time was in moral and spiritual darkness, people were driven by greed, intolerance and lust for power. Religion had become a device for the rich to rob the poor in the name of religion. Things haven't changed in the last 2000 years: greed, lust, power and money are still things that drive many people today. Just as the birth of Christ lit up the world on that night so many years ago, He still brings light and joy to people today who come to know Him as their Savior.

The Christmas season represents hope to a lost and dying world. Verse 17 above says the shepherds left to spread the word about what they had heard and seen. Can you imagine how excited they must have been to be part of the most exciting event in the history of the world? They saw the Son of God, the Messiah, the Savior of the world, and were given the privilege of spreading the news. A bunch of outcasts who weren't even allowed in the temple! I can just hear all the skeptics now saying, "They must be drunk, that's all they do you know, sit around out on the hills and get drunk." It is a classic example of God using the most unlikely people to spread the Word.

Verse 19 says that Mary treasured these things in her heart. Mary was probably thinking about all that had happened from the time the angel Gabriel appeared to her and told her she was going to give the birth to the Messiah, to it all culminating on that night. There she was, holding in her arms the most precious child that was ever born—and she had given birth to him!

She was probably thinking about the future and raising this child in her home. What an adventure! Raising the Son of God. Every parent thinks their kid is special, but Jesus really was in more ways than Mary and Joseph could even have imagined.

The birth of Christ represents the promise of forgiveness and joy in our hearts. Most of all, we are looking forward to the time when He comes again; this time in all of His glory, appearing in the clouds. Sadly, people who don't celebrate the birth of Christ will be very surprised when He comes again.

IT ALL BEGINS WITH CHRIST

ALL we like sheep have gone astray; we have turned every one to his own way; and the Lord hath laid on him the iniquity of us ALL.

Isaiah 53:7 KJV

It ALL begins and ends with Christ. ALL we have to do is follow him. It is that simple. People tend make being forgiven a lot harder than it is. They think there is some kind of restitution that needs to be paid and that is not the case at all, because Jesus Christ already paid the restitution on the cross for all of us. All we have to do is ask for his forgiveness and repent of our sins. It really is that simple, you don't have to do anything, it has already been done and he is waiting for you to ask. Then you will be welcomed with open arms and the angels will rejoice.

> *There is rejoicing in the presence of the angels of God over one sinner who repents.*
>
> Luke 15:10 NIV

IT'S TIME TO STAY AND SEEK CHRIST

> But I said, "I have labored in vain; I have spent my strength for nothing at all. Yet what is due me is in the Lord's hand, and my reward is with my God.
>
> Isaiah 49:4 NIV

Do you hear what the Lord is saying through Isaiah in this verse? He is saying that all of his efforts to lead people to redemption have been in vain, people weren't listening to him. They ignored him, blasphemed him, and crucified him, because they didn't believe him. The children of Israel wound up in captivity because they ignored Christ then, and people today are in captivity again. Not in a literal sense as being slaves to another nation, but they are slaves to all kinds of sinful behavior: lust, greed, sexual immorality, financial irresponsibility, and just plain ignoring God; all so that they can do their own thing.

God has raised up leaders in every generation to lead people back to Christ and show them the way, but in this generation, nobody has stepped up and accepted the mantle of telling the plain truth about Jesus Christ and the plan of salvation. The last great leader was Billy Graham. He led more people to Christ than anyone before him, through his crusades and via television. The remarkable thing is, he preached a very simple message of salvation and how to come to Christ. His messages were just plain good theology.

There are a lot of people preaching today who have mega churches, but they are not Billy Graham. So many preachers today are trying to be psychologists, preaching psychobabble to people about how to live a better life, instead of preaching on the basics of salvation, things like prayer and studying the Bible, and really seeking God in their lives. If people understand the basics, then everything else will fall into place. I read recently that a lot of preachers are afraid to preach about things like the end times and hell. They would rather try and preach messages about things that are pertinent to what is going on in people's lives than the message that Christ himself preached. Understand this: the closer you get to God, the less the problems in your life are worth worrying about. People in churches today need to get back to the basics

Jesus Christ summed up his reason for coming to this earth in these simple words:

> *For God so loved the world that he gave his one and only son, that whoever believes in him shall not perish, but have eternal life. For God did not send his son into the world to condemn the world, but to save the world through him. Whoever believes in him is not condemned, but whoever does not believe stands condemned already, because he has not believed in the name of the God's one and only son. This is the verdict: light has come into the world, but men loved darkness instead of light, because their deeds were evil. Everyone who does evil hates the light and will not come into the light for fear that his deeds will be exposed. But whoever lives by the truth comes into the light so that it may be seen plainly that what he has done has been done through God.*
>
> John 3:16–21 NIV

Whoever believes in him shall not perish, but have eternal life. Christ didn't come to condemn you for your sins, but to save you from them and to forgive you. Whoever doesn't believe is condemned already. Light has come into the world—Jesus Christ—but they rejected him and chose darkness and doing sinful things over living a life full of the light in Christ. Whoever lives by the truth comes into the light. Either you're living in the light, or you're living in darkness. There are no gray areas. Either you are serving God with all of your heart or you're not. Period. God cannot stand lukewarm Christians.

JESUS CHRIST WILL NEVER FAIL YOU

> *Keep your lives free from the love of money and be content with what you have, because God has said, "Never will I leave you; never will I forsake you.": so we say with confidence, "The Lord is my helper; I will not be afraid. What can mere mortals do to me?" Remember your leaders, who spoke the word of God to you. Consider the outcome of their way of life and imitate their faith. Jesus Christ is the same yesterday and today and forever. Do not be carried away by all kinds of strange teachings.*
>
> Hebrews 13:5–9 NIV

If you have lived very long in this world, you have seen a lot of changes. People come and go; politicians come and go. I have lived long enough to see us go from typewriters and faxes to high-speed internet, email and "air dropping" files. The Bible is not only the word of God, but it is also a history book. It tells how this world was formed by God and that Adam and Eve were the first human beings he created. It also tells the history of the Children of Israel and the lineage of Jesus Christ, from his miraculous birth to his death on the cross and his resurrection. He is still alive today and forever. Other religious leaders are dead. Mohammad, Buddha, Brigham Young and even Billy Graham are all dead; pastors of churches come and go. But Jesus said He will never leave us or forsake us, and He is the same yesterday, today. and tomorrow. His word and message are the same as they were 2000 years ago when he spoke them. Other religions and religious leaders have come and gone, along with a lot of strange ideas. Jesus isn't a religion.

He is the one and only Son of God. He is the only one you can depend on. He will always be there for you; His phone is never busy, and you don't have to make an appointment. He will listen to your prayers anytime. He knows your name and He knows when you were born and when you will die. If everyone else has failed you, try getting to know Jesus, He will never fail and He knows what you need before you ask. If you haven't read his biography, it is called the Bible and it has been a best seller for thousands of years. Pick up a copy and read it—your life will never be the same.

JESUS USE ME

> *For by grace you have been saved through faith, and that not of yourselves; it is the gift of God, not of works, lest anyone should boast. For we are His workmanship, created in Christ Jesus for good works, which God prepared beforehand that we should walk in them.*
>
> Ephesians 2:8–10 NKJV

Jesus will use you if you ask Him and are willing to do what He asks. Sometimes it may be something that you never would expect to be doing. I have talked to people who have said, "But how can God use me? I don't have any gifts or talents." The first step is to be willing and the second step is to do what He asks, no matter what. A lot of people miss opportunities to serve because they are not listening and not open to letting the Holy Spirit guide them. We have to quit trying to do things ourselves and let Him lead the way. He will guide you and help you be successful. After serving 23 years in the Army, I never in my wildest dreams thought I would ever be a hospice chaplain. I became an ordained minister and a pastor, then the Lord opened doors in ways that I never expected. It was my great privilege to pray with people who were nearing the end of their life and see them come to Christ or draw closer to him. God will use you too if just are willing to trust Him and let Him direct your path. There is no greater blessing than being used by God.

JOB, A TRUE MAN OF GOD

> *I will sing of the Lord's great love forever;*
> *with my mouth I will make your faithfulness known through all generations.*
> *I will declare that your love stands firm forever,*
> *that you established your faithfulness in heaven itself.*
>
> Psalm 89:1–2 NIV

The mark of a true Christian is being able to handle adversity and give the God the praise, no matter what is going on in your life. There is something about going through tough times and being able to look back and see God's hand in those things. Knowing that He is faithful is what keeps us going when we just want to give up and stay in bed in the morning.

Job lost his whole family, everything he owned was destroyed, he got very sick and had all kinds of physical problems, and to top it all off, his tender loving wife told him to curse God and die! There is nobody else who has ever gone through what Job did. God was bragging on Job and talking about what a great man he was. He was so faithful that nothing could make him turn his back on God. Satan and God made a wager between them. God told Satan that he could do anything he wanted to Job but kill him and Job would remain faithful to God.

> *I know that my Redeemer lives,*
> *and that in the end he will stand upon the earth.*
> *And after my skin has been destroyed,*
> *yet in my flesh I will see God;*
> *I myself will see him with my own eyes — I, and not another.*
> *How my heart yearns within me!*
>
> Job 19:25–27 NIV

Whether or not the story of Job is true, it is a great example of a man who literally lost everything he had, even his health. Job was the wealthiest man in the area and he had a lot to lose. He was not aware that he was being tested by God to see how much he could take. Job took everything Satan threw at him, but he knew that God was there with him.

When it was over, God replaced everything Job had lost and then some:

> *After Job had prayed for his friends, the Lord restored his fortunes and*
> *gave him twice as much as he had before. All his brothers and sisters and*
> *everyone who had known him before came and ate with him in his house.*
> *They comforted and consoled him over all the trouble the Lord had brought*
> *on him, and each one gave him a piece of silver and a gold ring.*
> *The Lord blessed the latter part of Job's life more than the former part. He*
> *had fourteen thousand sheep, six thousand camels, a thousand yoke of oxen*
> *and a thousand donkeys. And he also had seven sons and three daughters.*
> *The first daughter he named Jemimah, the second Keziah and the third*
> *Keren-Happuch. Nowhere in all the land were there found women as beau-*
> *tiful as Job's daughters, and their father granted them an inheritance along*
> *with their brothers. After this, Job lived a hundred and forty years; he saw*

his children and their children to the fourth generation. And so Job died, an
old man and full of years.

Job 42:10–17 NIV

The inspiration and courage that Job had through all of the things he went through shows us that God will always be there when we need him, even during the toughest times in our lives. God's people have went through a lot of horrors in the last several thousand years and He has always been there and taken a lot of people to be in heaven with Him.

We may not be able to see God, but rest assured, He is always with you.

JOY IN TIMES OF TROUBLE

> *Though the fig tree does not bud and there are no grapes on the vines, though the olive crop fails and the fields produce no food, though there are no sheep in the pen and no cattle in the stalls, yet I will rejoice in the Lord, I will be joyful in God my Savior.*
>
> Habakkuk 3:17–18 NIV

Today, are you feeling like everything is going wrong and there is no hope in sight? Habakkuk tells us to be joyful anyway and give praise to God. It is in times of trouble that we feel closest to God and receive our greatest blessings. Don't give up! God will never fail you and He is always right on time.

Trusting God during the difficult times in your life is very hard to do. We have a tendency to pray and say we are giving it all to Him and then we take it back and try to work things out ourselves. It is during those times when we are tested the most about whether we really trust God or not.

A lot of times we come to the end of our rope and realize that giving it all to God is the only way to solve our problems. We have to remember that God's timing is not our timing; His ways are not our ways. That is where the trusting part comes in and we just have to wait on God to move and work in His time. In the meantime, we have to continue to give Him praise and worship Him no matter what is going on around us.

JUSTIFYING EVIL FOR PERSONAL GAIN

Woe to those who call evil good and good evil,
who put darkness for light and light for darkness,
who put bitter for sweet and sweet for bitter.
Woe to those who are wise in their own eyes
and clever in their own sight.
Woe to those who are heroes at drinking wine
and champions at mixing drinks,
who acquit the guilty for a bribe,
but deny justice to the innocent.

Isaiah 5:20–23 NIV

This scripture was written thousands of years ago but applies today more than ever. People are twisting the truth and telling outright lies for their own personal gain. Innocent babies are being killed while in the womb and there are those would kill them as soon as they are born.

Some people are so convinced they are right, they are blinded by evil. It doesn't matter what your political beliefs are, it is your spiritual beliefs and relationship with Jesus Christ that matter.

Whenever I read this scripture, I think about the events of September 11, 2001, and what a horrible day that was. America was under attack on our own soil. The churches were packed the first few Sundays and young men and women were enlisting the Armed Forces in record numbers. But it didn't take long for people to act as if nothing had happened and were back to their normal activities. People have very short memories, and some are denying September 11, 2001 even happened. It is up to us as Christians to be ever on alert. September 11, 2001 was a wakeup call to America to always be vigilant and alert for another attack on America.

Wake up America and call on God once again. He is our only hope.

LEARN FROM YESTERDAY

"Learn from Yesterday, Live for Today, Hope for Tomorrow."

Albert Einstein

Have you ever heard anyone say life is too short?

Well it is true. No matter how long you live, whether you live to be 40 or 80, there are always things left to do. That is why it is important to live each day of your life as if it is your last.

> *Do every good work, growing in the knowledge of God, being strengthened with all power according to his glorious might so that you may have great endurance and patience, and giving joyful thanks to the Father, who has qualified you to share in the inheritance of his holy people in the kingdom of light.*
>
> Colossians 1:10–12 NIV

Our main purpose in life is to serve the Lord, and that is where many of us get off track. Instead of listening to Him, we tend to go our own way. We spend time making bucket lists instead of spending time with the Lord. And His word.

There is nothing wrong with having a bucket list. I understand having a list of things you would like to do and see while you are here, still healthy. Keeping God in the equation is also very important. Go and see the things on your list but also keep up a daily regimen of prayer and bible reading, or devotions.

God has a way of changing our plans. One time my wife and I were on our way to Yellowstone Park to see Yogi Bear and his friends when we got a call from her Mom saying that her Dad was in the hospital in critical condition. So we kept on going, right past Yellowstone to Lake Havasu City, Arizona, where we spent the month of August instead of exploring Yellowstone.

> *The Lord had said to Abram, "Go from your country, your people and your father's household to the land I will show you. I will make you into a great nation, and I will bless you; I will make your name great, and you will be a blessing. I will bless those who bless you, and whoever curses you I will curse; and all peoples on earth will be blessed through you."*
>
> Genesis 12:1-3 NIV

Always be willing to change your plans as God leads. Remember, serving the Lord isn't a chore that should be done grudgingly, but done with joy. Always include God in everything you do and everywhere you go, using the gifts he has given you. So be diligent, be read up, be prayed up and always serving for the Lord.

LIBERTY

> *For you, brethren, have been called to liberty; only do not use liberty as an opportunity for the flesh, but through love serve one another.*
>
> Galatians 5:13 NKJV

Where there is liberty, there is freedom. Some people use that freedom for their own selfish desires. Real freedom comes from helping others and giving whatever we have freely. The Fourth of July is about celebrating our freedom as a nation and freedom from religious intolerance. We have the freedom to worship and live as we choose. Pray that we are able to maintain that freedom and the liberty we have.

There is a lot of fear in the United States today that we are losing the freedoms we cherish, such as being able to worship where we choose. It seems that everything is in chaos and the price of just about everything keeps going up. There are people who deny that this nation was founded by Godly people who were seeking religious freedom. There is plenty of evidence to prove the Pilgrims first came to America to get away from religious persecution. The only way to keep those liberties is to continue to pray and go to church. There may come a time when all Christian people will have to stand up to oppression once again in order to keep our freedoms. We must not let our guard down and turn the other way. The enemy would like nothing more than to see all churches closed in America and people be forced meet in secret like in China and Russia. God will not abandon us and He will be victorious, but we also have be willing to fight for those freedoms just like our ancestors did.

LIFE IS TOO SHORT

> Show me, Lord, my life's end
> and the number of my days;
> let me know how fleeting my life is.
> You have made my days a mere handbreadth;
> the span of my years is as nothing before you.
> Everyone is but a breath
>
> Psalm 39:4–5 NIV

Are you so busy that you forget to make time to do the little things in life that are so important? Hurrying is accepted as the way we are supposed to do things in American life. People are so anxious to get on with whatever they have to do, they forget to make time for relationships. When hurrying becomes a chronic condition, we run even when there is no reason. We rush while performing even the most mundane tasks. We have become addicted to hurrying. Despite all of this rushing around, hurry-sick people are still not satisfied. So out of desperation, we find ourselves doing more than one thing at a time. There is even a scientific name for it: Polyphasic activity, better known as multitasking. The car is a favorite place to do this. People may drive, eat, drink coffee, monitor the radio, shave or apply make-up, talk on their cell phone and make gestures all at the same time. These type of people have a day planner the size of an encyclopedia.

Life is too short to let your life be dictated by all these things you think are so important. Time waits for no man; that person you have been putting off visiting may be gone tomorrow. We have no way of knowing what tomorrow is going to bring and putting off the things in life that are really important could be a big mistake—one you regret the rest of your life. Your job is never going to give you the fulfillment that spending time with those you love and care about will. Today is the first day of the rest of your life. Start living it wisely.

Maybe this prayer rings true for you:

The clock is my dictator, I shall not rest.
It makes me lie down only when exhausted.
It leads me into deep depression
It hounds my soul.
It leads me in circles of frenzy, for activities' sake.
Even though I run frantically from task to task I will never get it all done
For my ideal is with me
Deadlines and my need for approval, they drive me.
They demand performance from me, beyond the limits of my schedule.
They anoint my head with migraines.
My in-basket overflows
Surely fatigue and time pressures shall follow me
All the days of my life.
And I will dwell in the bonds of frustration forever.

Marcia K. Hornok

LIFE THROUGH DEATH

Who has believed our message and to whom has the arm of the Lord been revealed? He grew up before him like a tender shoot, and like a root out of dry ground. He had no beauty or majesty to attract us to him, nothing in his appearance that we should desire him. He was despised and rejected by men, a man of sorrows, and familiar with suffering. Like one from whom men hide their faces he was despised, and we esteemed him not. Surely he took up our infirmities and carried our sorrows, yet we considered him stricken by God, smitten by him, and afflicted. But he was pierced for our transgressions, he was crushed for our iniquities; the punishment that brought us peace was upon him, and by his wounds we are healed. We all, like sheep, have gone astray, each of us has turned to his own way; and the Lord has laid on him the iniquity of us all.

Isaiah 53:1–6 NIV84

Jesus read these scriptures and knew he had been born to die for the sins of the world. We don't know exactly at what age he fully understood this was going to be his destiny, but I can't even imagine knowing at the age of twelve what I was going to be facing, and how I was going to die. I think God is merciful in not letting us see the future. What if you knew at the age of twelve what your life was going to be like and that you were going to be ridiculed and doubted by your own friends and family? You were going to be tried unjustly and found guilty, whipped, and beaten to point of being barely alive, then hung on a cross to die. Would you be willing to do that? Most people would probably be severely depressed and even suicidal. People today think they have problems they can't handle. Our problems are nothing compared to what Christ went through in his life here on earth for us. You are not ready to live until you are ready to die. Christ died so that we could live and have the knowledge that He would be with us and ready to help us through whatever we face in this life.

LISTENING AND DOING

The Lord says, "Family of Jacob, listen to me. Pay attention, you people of Israel who are left alive. I have taken good care of you since your life began. I have carried you since you were born as a nation. I will continue to carry you even when you are old. I will take good care of you even when your hair is gray. I have made you, and I will carry you. I will take care of you, and I will save you.
I am the Lord."

Isaiah 46:3–4 NIrV

God will care for us and comfort us, no matter what happens. He said He would comfort Zion. He will make her wilderness like Eden, and her desert like the garden of the Lord. Joy and Gladness will be found there. There will be lovely songs of thanksgiving.

All God really wants is for us to worship Him and obey His laws. When we start thinking we can do things on our own, we get in trouble. That's what the Children of Israel did and they wound up in captivity. Today, people are doing the exact same thing; they are in bondage to all kinds of sin and worldly pleasures. The people were looking at their surroundings and getting discouraged and forgot everything God had done for them. God had prospered and blessed Israel. In their prosperity, they forgot God and trusted in their own strength. When people become prosperous, they tend to develop a false sense of security. They forget that God was the one who gave them the ability to prosper. People tend to look at God and say, "What have you done for me lately?"

Now, the Children of Israel were in trouble and discouraged, and couldn't see beyond their own problems. God is telling them that things are going to change. Truly obeying and following the Lord requires a lot of patience. He will do what needs to be done, but He will do it in His own time and at the right place.

LIVING A HOLY LIFE

> *Therefore, since we are surrounded by such a great cloud of witnesses, let us throw off everything that hinders and the sin that so easily entangles. And let us run with perseverance the race marked out for us, fixing our eyes on Jesus, the pioneer and perfecter of faith. For the joy set before him he endured the cross, scorning its shame, and sat down at the right hand of the throne of God. Consider him who endured such opposition from sinners, so that you will not grow weary and lose heart.*
>
> Hebrews 12:1–3 NIV

People talk about holiness and living a holy life. But what does that mean? According to Webster, holiness is the quality or state of being holy. How do we do that? Is it possible to live a holy life, and still be human? Holiness doesn't seek to be God; holiness seeks to be *like* God. When you accept Jesus Christ as your Savior, you receive His holiness and His Holy Spirit, by His grace. It is not a one-time transaction; this is a daily, moment by moment, way of life, striving to live more by the spirit and less by the flesh. Holiness is like a gift already purchased for us, by the blood of Christ. But we cannot have full use of it until a certain date in the future, when we will go to heaven and be glorified in Christ. We live in a sin filled world and it is impossible not to sin. Many times, we sin and don't even realize it. Whenever you put yourself under a doctor's care, he can't help you if you don't follow his instructions. As the patient surrenders his will and listens to the doctor, he becomes well. God is the doctor in this case and through His Holy Spirit, He helps us not to sin and warns us when temptation knocks on our door. If we want to be made holy, we must willingly surrender ourselves to His care and actively obey His instructions. We have no more power to make ourselves holy than a dying man has to save himself. We are weak and tired and can't offer much help, unless we submit to His rehab program. The key to our part is faith. To seek Him in obedience. His prescription is the Bible and as we study it, we learn how God wants us to live. We are going to have moments where we are severely tempted, and we have go to the Lord in prayer and ask forgiveness. We will never be completely holy until we get to heaven, and we are purified by God and have brand new heavenly bodies and a different way of thinking. The best thing we can do is try to live a holy life with the help of the Holy Spirit. People will know you are a follower of Christ by your actions and your demeanor. That is the best witness you can have because people will be watching you and there will be times you can talk to your friends and coworkers about Christ because they will be curious about what is different about you. That is simple: You are a child of God, and your body is the temple of the Holy Spirit.

LIVING IN GOD'S HOUSE

The Lord is my light and my salvation;
Whom shall I fear?
The Lord is the strength of my life;
Of whom shall I be afraid?
When the wicked came against me to eat up my flesh,
My enemies and foes, They stumbled and fell,
My heart shall not fear;
Though an army may encamp against me,
My heart shall not fear;
Though war may rise against me,
In this I will be confident.
One thing I have desired of the Lord, That will I seek:
That I may dwell in the house of the Lord All the days of my life,
To behold the beauty of the Lord,
And to inquire in His temple.
For in the time of trouble He shall hide me in His pavilion;
In the secret place of His tabernacle He shall hide me;
He shall set me high upon a rock.

Psalm 27:1–5 NKJV

If you could ask God for one thing, what would you ask for? A long life? Good health? Riches? Fame?

David tells us what he would ask. He longs to live in the house of God. I emphasize the word "live," because it deserves to be emphasized.

David doesn't want to chat. He doesn't desire a cup of coffee on the back porch. He doesn't ask for a meal or to spend an evening in God's house. He longs to retire there. He doesn't seek a temporary assignment but rather lifelong residence.

David said in Psalm 23:6, "I will live in the house of the Lord forever." He's saying simply that he never wants to step away from God. He craves to remain in the aura, in the atmosphere, in the awareness that he is in God's house, wherever he is.

Most people haven't learned to dwell in God's house. We may visit, stop in for the day, even stay for a meal. But abide? This is God's desire.

Listen to the words of Jesus:

> *Jesus answered and said to him, "If anyone loves Me, he will keep My word; and My Father will love him, and We will come to him and make Our home with him. He who does not love Me does not keep My words; and the word which you hear is not Mine but the Father's who sent Me.*
> John 14:23–24 NKJV

Deep inside every man there is a private place that is the very essence of his being—it is called the soul. The soul is a gift from God, whom man is dependent upon for his very existence. Living in the house of God should be every Christian's main desire; to worship our Lord and savior all the time. We don't know what the house of God or heaven will look like exactly, but we do know it will be the most beautiful, glorious place we have ever seen. So Wonderful that words can't describe it.

This life is about living the best we know how for the Lord and serving Him here on this earth. Heaven will be a reward for all the work for him we have done here on earth.

For behold, I create new heavens and a new earth;
And the former shall not be remembered or come to mind.
But be glad and rejoice forever in what I create;
For behold, I create Jerusalem as a rejoicing,
And her people a joy.
I will rejoice in Jerusalem,
And joy in My people;
The voice of weeping shall no longer be heard in her,
Nor the voice of crying.
No more shall an infant from there live but a few days,
Nor an old man who has not fulfilled his days;
For the child shall die one hundred years old,
But the sinner being one hundred years old shall be accursed.
They shall build houses and inhabit them;
They shall plant vineyards and eat their fruit.
They shall not build and another inhabit;
They shall not plant and another eat;
For as the days of a tree, so shall be the days of My people,
And My elect shall long enjoy the work of their hands.
They shall not labor in vain,
Nor bring forth children for trouble;
For they shall be the descendants of the blessed of the Lord,
And their offspring with them.
                                        Isaiah 65:17–23 NKJV

Knowing we are going to die and wake up in heaven makes this life more tolerable. Knowing that all of the pain and sorrow will be forgotten, and we have a glorious future ahead of us in heaven—a wonderful thing to look forward to—is more than words can describe.

LIVING IN THE SPIRIT WITH LOVE

> *For you, brethren, have been called to liberty; only do not use liberty as an opportunity for the flesh, but through love serve one another. For all the law is fulfilled in one word, even in this: "You shall love your neighbor as yourself." But if you bite and devour one another, beware lest you be consumed by one another! I say then: Walk in the Spirit, and you shall not fulfill the lust of the flesh. For the flesh lusts against the Spirit, and the Spirit against the flesh; and these are contrary to one another, so that you do not do the things that you wish. But if you are led by the Spirit, you are not under the law.*
>
> Galatians 5:13–18 NKJV

Trying to walk in the Spirit and be obedient, to do what the Lord would have us do in obedience to him, can be a very hard thing to do in the world we live in today.

When the Apostle Paul talks about the law, he is talking about the Jewish law that the scribes and the Pharisees had declared would be the law everyone was to live under. It had become an unwieldy document, with hundreds of laws that nobody could comply with fully.

Paul was saying that Christ had come and died for our sins to free us from the law, to live in the Spirit and be free; living the way Christ would have us to live. Every day each of us should ask the Holy Spirit to help us live the way Christ would have us to live. Satan is in a battle every day for your soul, and the temptation to live in the flesh is all around us. That is why every day we must die to self and live for Christ. Satan knows his time is getting short, and he is fighting harder and more fiercely than ever before to take as many people with him when, at the end of time, he will be thrown into the lake of fire.

Every morning, pray that God will surround you with his angels and clothe you in the Armor of God, protecting you from all the tricks Satan has in his bag to lure you away from Christ. Jesus loves you and He wants you to share that love with everyone you come in contact with, every single day.

LOVE CONQUERS ALL

> *Though I speak with the tongues of men and of angels, but have not love, I have become sounding brass or a clanging cymbal. And though I have the gift of prophecy, and understand all mysteries and all knowledge, and though I have all faith, so that I could remove mountains, but have not love, I am nothing. And though I bestow all my goods to feed the poor, and though I give my body to be burned, but have not love, it profits me nothing.*
>
> 1 Corinthians 13:1–3 NKJV

Many people believe this is the greatest chapter in the New Testament, and with good reason. Paul begins by telling us that we may possess a spiritual gift, but unless we have the gift of love it is useless. We may have the gift of speaking in tongues, but without love it is just a lot of confusing noise. Because when someone speaks in tongues, they are praising and worshiping God and showing their love for Him. Whenever the interpretation is given of a word spoken in tongues, there is always an undercurrent of God showing His love for us. Some may have the gift of prophecy. Most people think that prophecy is foretelling a future event. That is not necessarily true. Prophecy is the gift that corresponds most closely to preaching. Prophecy means to speak out. Whenever you witness to someone and tell them about the love of Jesus, you are prophesying. There are two kinds of preachers: Those who try to bring people into the kingdom of God by telling them how much God loves them and cares about them; and those who preach hellfire and damnation. The latter try to scare people into heaven. God is not an ill-tempered father who slaps us around every time we get out of line. The God I know loves us and gently corrects us through His Holy Spirit. Some people may have the gift of intellectual knowledge; they are very intelligent people who can quote the Bible better than some preachers and can argue a biblical point forever. People who do that without love are intellectual snobs. Talking about the Bible in a cold and detached manner, without talking about the love of Christ, is about as effective as reading the encyclopedia to someone. They gain a lot of knowledge, but they don't get anything out of it. Some may practice charity by giving to others. Charity without love is like giving scraps to a stray dog. If we look down on those who are less fortunate than we are, and give out of a sense of duty, rather than a spirit of compassion, that's not love—that is passing judgment. Many Christians tend to treat those who are unsaved as somehow being less a person than they are. Jesus said, "Let him who is without sin, cast the first stone." Jesus never turned anyone away because they did not look or act as He did.

LOVE ONE ANOTHER

> *And this is his command: to believe in the name of his Son, Jesus Christ, and to love one another as he commanded us. The one who keeps God's commands lives in him, and he in them. And this is how we know that he lives in us: We know it by the Spirit he gave us.*
>
> 1 John 3:23 NIV

Here John gives us the two main points of Jesus ministry: to believe Jesus is the Son of God, and to love each other as Christ loves us. The love Jesus shows us transcends all races, classes, and sexes. Jesus doesn't care who you are or what you have done in your life. He loves you in spite of yourself! All He asks is that you believe in Him and love others in spite of who or what they are. We tend look at others with a critical eye and judge them by their outward appearance or actions. Jesus looks at the heart and He sees who we really are—and what we could be if we only put our faith and trust in Him. Jesus never turned anyone away because of their appearance or how they were dressed. Jesus Himself only had one set of clothes and had no home; He slept wherever He could, even outside if He wasn't invited to spend the night somewhere. That is why He did not spend a lot of time with religious leaders of the day, because He wanted everyone to know that He loved and accepted everyone. His only requirement was that they believe He is the Son of God and that He can forgive them from their sins. Our job isn't to judge people, it is to tell people about Jesus and let Him be the judge and offer them forgiveness of their sins.

MEDITATING ON SCRIPTURE

> *Blessed is the man*
> *Who walks not in the counsel of the ungodly,*
> *Nor stands in the path of sinners,*
> *Nor sits in the seat of the scornful;*
> *But his delight is in the law of the Lord,*
> *And in His law he meditates day and night.*
> *He shall be like a tree*
> *Planted by the rivers of water,*
> *That brings forth its fruit in its season,*
> *Whose leaf also shall not wither;*
> *And whatever he does shall prosper.*
>
> Psalm 1:1–3 NKJV

When we meditate on a scripture, it means we are totally focused on what we are reading and what it is saying to us. In order to do that, we must prepare our hearts in order to receive what the Holy Spirit will reveal. We need to anticipate that He will speak to us as we read. "May the words of my mouth and the meditation of my heart be pleasing in your sight." Let's think about what that means for a minute. In order to hear from God, we need to find a quiet place and clear our minds of everything and listen for the voice of the Holy Spirit. We need to do the same thing when we are meditating on scripture. Before we start reading, we should ask God to help us focus and remove any unwanted thoughts from our mind, purifying our hearts in order to receive from God's word. That includes asking forgiveness if we need to, and not let our own thoughts interrupt the work of the Holy Spirit. It is hard to concentrate on scripture when you have a thousand other things going through your mind. **We should meditate on His Word day and night.** This is where scripture memorization is so important, so we can recall God's word as we are going through our day. Many times when I am reading, God will reveal a certain verse to me and I will think about it the rest of the day.

Let the words of my mouth and the meditation of my heart
Be acceptable in Your sight,
O Lord, my strength and my Redeemer.

Psalm 19:14 NKJV

Meditating on scripture is not the same thing as just reading the Bible. If you read the Bible just for information and knowledge and don't expect anything else, that is what you will get. Many people have read the Bible and know what it says better than some preachers, but they have never meditated on it and applied it to their lives. If you read the Bible like you would a novel, you may come away thinking it is a great story and has a lot of wisdom in it but may not necessarily feel it applies to you. I like to read old western novels for pleasure because it is easy reading, and I don't have to think about what the book is saying—I just enjoy the story. I don't expect to read anything really profound that will change my life. Many people have picked up a Bible for the first time and started reading out of curiosity but were open to what it said and their lives were changed. Jesus talked about people who read the scripture and are not changed by it or not open to letting it speak to their hearts.

You search the Scriptures, for in them you think you have eternal life; and these are they which testify of Me. But you are not willing to come to Me that

you may have life. I do not receive honor from men. But I know you, that
you do not have the love of God in you. I have come in My Father's name,
and you do not receive Me; if another comes in his own name, him you will
receive. How can you believe, who receive honor from one another, and do
not seek the honor that comes from the only God?

John 5:39–44 NKJV

The truth is we are all trapped in a world where our minds are bombarded with things that are not consistent with living the life that Christ would have us live and memorizing and meditating on key scriptures that really speak to us and help shield us from the fiery darts of Satan. It is all part of putting on the Armor of God every day (see Ephesians Chapter 6:10–18).

We have to purposely set aside time for meditating on God's Word every day in order for Him to recognize us.

MERCY AND FORGIVENESS

> *For as the heaven is high above the earth,*
> *so great is his mercy toward them that fear him.*
> *As far as the east is from the west,*
> *so far hath he removed our transgressions from us.*
>
> Psalm 103:11–12 KJV

It is hard to grasp the imagery in this verse: Our sins being forgiven as far as the east is from the west and as far as heaven is from the earth. I am still amazed at watching astronauts take off and go into the sky so high they are out of the atmosphere and, as many times as I flown in aircraft, I still am in awe of how a commercial aircraft takes off and stays in the sky. That is nothing compared to how far our sins are forgiven and forgotten.

God created the world we live in and He can certainly forgive your sins and remove them so they will never be brought up by Him again.

It is a little harder for us to do that—and really mean it. I have heard people say, "I will forgive, but I will never forget." That isn't what God is telling us to do. As hard as it is to do sometimes, we have do as God commands us. You will find that a weight has been lifted off your shoulders by forgiving and forgetting, because it is now in God's hands. God loved you enough to forgive you, and you need be able to do the same with others. You will feel so much better, because whatever was is now gone, and God's love will surround you.

Thank you, Father, for your mercy upon us and for Your forgiveness of our sins; that they may never be remembered again.

MYSTERIES OF LIFE

I have been doing a lot of thinking lately about how fast life tends to go by and the fact that some people live longer than others. I remember wanting to grow up faster and it seems like I was in high school forever. Then when I became an adult and was very busy working and raising a family, it seemed like time flew by and I wished I was a kid again playing with my friends and not a care in the world. I am thankful that I had a good childhood; my parents did their best to provide for me. They weren't rich but we didn't go hungry either. So many people never had the privilege of having a good childhood or living a long life, for many reasons like sickness or accidents.

There are two scriptures that tell us if we trust in the Lord and let Him guide us, life will be better:

> *Trust in the Lord with all your heart,*
> *And lean not on your own understanding;*
> *In all your ways acknowledge Him,*
> *And He shall direct your paths.*
> *Do not be wise in your own eyes;*
> *Fear the Lord and depart from evil.*

It will be health to your flesh,
And strength to your bones.

Proverbs 3:5–7 NKJV

For I know the thoughts that I think toward you, says the Lord, thoughts of peace and not of evil, to give you a future and a hope. Then you will call upon Me and go and pray to Me, and I will listen to you. And you will seek Me and find Me, when you search for Me with all your heart. I will be found by you.

Jeremiah 29:11–14 NKJV

When I look back on my life now, I can see where the Lord was with me even during the times that I ignored the urging of the Holy Spirit and did things my own way. In spite of my many failures, the Lord always seemed to turn me around and lead me in the right direction. The Lord has blessed me in spite of myself and I can say thank you Lord for the life you have given me. And when my days on this earth are over, I can say that I had a good life and was truly blessed.

NEVER GIVE UP

> *Trust in the Lord with all thine heart; and lean not unto thine own understanding. In all thy ways acknowledge him, and he shall direct thy paths.*
>
> Proverbs 3:5–6 KJV

I have faced a lot of health issues these last couple of years, and I confess I have even thought of giving up at times and just asking the Lord to take me home.

But through it all, God has been faithful and—in spite of my failing health—has used me despite my own doubts and fears. I have been privileged to walk with our pastor over these last few years during some of the darkest times in the history of our church and have seen him grow from a new senior pastor, one who was literally thrown into the fire and faced a lot of discord within the church, into one of the best pastors and leaders in the White Mountains. I can vividly remember a time in November of 2017 when I was in the hospital and had just had major surgery to remove half of my colon due to a twisted large intestine. On the second day after surgery, our pastor came into the hospital room and said he was very much in need of prayer. We have since often joked about the fact that I was the guy in the hospital bed recovering from major surgery, yet our pastor came in saying he needed prayer instead of the other way around! We had a good time of prayer and fellowship that night, and Pastor said that during my prayer I said something very profound; something he needed to hear. I have no recollection of what I said, because I was on some pretty heavy drugs, but it goes to show that God was using me through the Holy Spirit to minister to him in his time of need—even when I didn't know what I was saying!

Though I have not been active recently in the church and have—for the most part—been missing in action, God is still using me in ways that I could never have imagined; through people that have come to my home to do things around the house for Kathy and me, and even through my occasional blogs on Facebook. God is not finished with me yet and I really believe that God can use us wherever we are, regardless of our circumstances.

Today, under the leadership of our senior pastor, our church is experiencing the power of the Holy Spirit in our services like never before and is leading us into an exciting time of growth in ministry, and in the lives of our people. It doesn't matter who you are or where you are, God will open doors for you to have an opportunity of ministry; one that you will never see coming. Trusting in God with all of your heart and not leaning on your own understanding gives God the opportunity to work in your life. In other words, get out of the way and let God be God. That is probably the biggest obstacle in our lives; getting in God's way and not letting Him work.

NO CONDEMNATION

> *For all have sinned and fall short of the glory of God, and all are justified freely by his grace through the redemption that came by Christ Jesus.*
>
> Romans 3:23 NIV

In this era of rushing to judgment and accusing others of committing sins, it is good to remember what Jesus told those who accused the woman who was caught in the act of adultery: "Let any one of you who is without sin be the first to throw a stone at her." (John 8:7b NIV)

The Bible tells us that we all are guilty of sin and it is only by the grace of God that we can be forgiven. Thank God that our redemption comes by the blood of Jesus Christ, not at the hands of man!

> *Therefore, there is now no condemnation for those who are in Christ Jesus, because through Christ Jesus the law of the Spirit who gives life has set you free from the law of sin and death.*
>
> Romans 8:1–2 NIV

NO EYE HAS SEEN NOR EAR HEARD

When you open the door of your heart to the things of God, the Holy Spirit reveals things to you that you could not otherwise know. That is why people who have not asked Jesus to come into their heart and their life do not understand how God works, and the Bible is foolishness to them. It is only by being sensitive to the prompting of the Holy Spirit that you draw closer to God and are able to do things God would have you to do.

Psalm 46:10 says: Be still and know that I am God. Unless you get still and put everything out of your mind, you won't hear the Holy Spirit. The Holy Spirit doesn't shout at us.

> *The person without the Spirit does not accept the things that come from the Spirit of God but considers them foolishness, and cannot understand them because they are discerned only through the Spirit.*
>
> 1 Corinthians 2:14 NIV

We get so busy trying to figure out a problem on our own that we forget to listen to the voice of the Holy Spirit telling us we are not making the right decisions.

NOBODY IS PERFECT

> *For we all stumble in many things. If anyone does not stumble in word, he is a perfect man, able also to bridle the whole body. Indeed, we put bits in horses' mouths that they may obey us, and we turn their whole body. Look also at ships: although they are so large and are driven by fierce winds, they are turned by a very small rudder wherever the pilot desires. Even so the tongue is a little member and boasts great things.*
>
> James 3:2–5a NKJV

I often hear of people who leave a particular church because of something someone else in the church said or did, and it strikes me that it doesn't matter what church you attend, people are going to say or do something to offend you. That is because we all tend say things that cannot be taken back. Our tongue can be our best friend or our worst enemy, and just because we go to church, it doesn't necessarily make our speech any better or kinder than anyone else. The next time someone in the church says something that offends you, just remember that we all struggle with what we say sometimes, and we all are sinners saved by grace, in spite of our speech and our actions. Sometimes a little grace and forgiveness can go a long way towards getting along with our Christian brothers and sisters.

OBTAINING SPIRITUAL MATURITY

> *We have much to say about this, which is hard to explain, since you have grown lazy about learning. For though you ought to be teachers by now, you need someone to teach you the elementary principles of God's word again. It has come to the point where you are in need of milk, not solid food, for everyone who lives on milk stays unskilled in the word of righteousness, since he remains a child. But solid food is for the mature, for those who have had their abilities of discernment trained by exercise in order to be able to distinguish good from evil.*
>
> *Hebrews 5:11–14 Lifegate*

The author of Hebrews is saying that there comes a time when you have to get beyond the basics of Christianity and start growing and maturing in your Christian walk. It is not enough just to know you are saved and have been baptized and have the hope of eternal life in heaven. You have to grow and mature just as a child does; you do that by eating solid food and by learning something new every day. If you spent your whole life just drinking milk and never going to school or leaving your house, you would be very immature, uneducated and malnourished.

OF ONE ACCORD

> *Therefore if there is any consolation in Christ, if any comfort of love, if any fellowship of the Spirit, if any affection and mercy, fulfill my joy by being like-minded, having the same love, being of one accord, of one mind. Let nothing be done through selfish ambition or conceit, but in lowliness of mind let each esteem others better than himself. Let each of you look out not only for his own interests, but also for the interests of others.*
>
> Philippians 2:1–9 NKJV

Selfishness can ruin a church. Many people, even Christians, live only to make a good impression on others, or to please others. Selfishness brings spiritual discord. That is exactly what God doesn't want—but Satan does. Paul stressed spiritual unity, asking people to love one another and to be one in spirit and purpose. If we are of one accord, even the gates of hell cannot prevail against us. Genuine humility and selflessness will build a church, more than anything. People will know whether we are real, or just putting on a good show on Sunday morning.

ONLY ONE NAME UNDER HEAVEN

> *Therefore I exhort first of all that supplications, prayers, intercessions, and giving of thanks be made for all men, for kings and all who are in authority, that we may lead a quiet and peaceable life in all godliness and reverence. For this is good and acceptable in the sight of God our Savior, who desires all men to be saved and to come to the knowledge of the truth. For there is one God and one Mediator between God and men, the Man Christ Jesus, who gave Himself a ransom for all, to be testified in due time.*
>
> 1 Timothy 2:1–5 NKJV

It is important to remember that Jesus Christ is Lord, and one day every knee shall bow, and every tongue confess that Jesus is Lord. He alone is the one we should put our trust in and know that He is really the one in charge, no matter what happens. It doesn't matter who is in the White House; God is still in charge, even though sometimes it doesn't seem like it. Our job is to pray for our leaders, not judge them. Pray that those who know Christ will be sensitive to the Holy Spirit speaking in their hearts, and those that don't will accept Christ and be the responsible leaders we elected.

OUR HELPER IS ALWAYS NEAR

But we have this treasure in jars of clay to show that this all-surpassing power is from God and not from us. We are hard pressed on every side, but not crushed; perplexed, but not in despair; persecuted, but not abandoned; struck down, but not destroyed. We always carry around in our body the death of Jesus, so that the life of Jesus may also be revealed in our body. For we who are alive are always being given over to death for Jesus' sake, so that his life may also be revealed in our mortal body. So then, death is at work in us, but life is at work in you. It is written: "I believed; therefore I have spoken." Since we have that same spirit of faith, we also believe and therefore speak, because we know that the one who raised the Lord Jesus from the dead will also raise us with Jesus and present us with you to himself. All this is for your benefit, so that the grace that is reaching more and more people may cause thanksgiving to overflow to the glory of God. Therefore we do not lose heart. Though outwardly we are wasting away, yet inwardly we are being renewed day by day. For our light and momentary troubles are achieving for us an eternal glory that far outweighs them all. So we fix our eyes not on what is seen, but on what is unseen, since what is seen is temporary, but what is unseen is eternal.

2 Corinthians 4:7–18 NIV

The apostle Paul suffered for the cause of Christ, probably as much as anyone in the Bible. He was beaten, flogged, thrown in prison, stoned, and gladly suffered all those things because he knew that Christ was with him, and he would soon be with Christ in heaven. I wonder how many of us would be willing to go through what Paul did and stay faithful to Christ. There are people all over the world being persecuted because they will not renounce Christ. We are fortunate here in the United States. We are still able to worship as we please and not suffer for it like Paul did.

People today are able to withstand the persecution they are going through just like Paul did, because they have the Holy Spirit with them to give them strength and courage. Jesus said he would never leave us or forsake us even in the worst of times. He is with you right now and will be with you no matter what happens. Jesus is Lord of all and always will be.

OUR WANDERING MINDS

> *What is causing the quarrels and fights among you? Don't they come from the evil desires at war within you? You want what you don't have, so you scheme and kill to get it. You are jealous of what others have, but you can't get it, so you fight and wage war to take it away from them. Yet you don't have what you want because you don't ask God for it. And even when you ask, you don't get it because your motives are all wrong—you want only what will give you pleasure.*
>
> James 4:1–3 NLT

John Milton said, "The mind is owned of the self. It can make a hell of heaven or a heaven of hell."[1] He was right that the things we think about determine the kind of life we live and can cause us to be either happy or miserable.

The Bible also has a lot to say about the mind and what we think about:

---

1. John Milton, Paradise Lost

The mind governed by the flesh is death, but the mind governed by the Spirit is life and peace.

Romans 8:6 NIV

The mind can be the devil's playground if we let it, destroying our relationship with Christ. It is very important to stay focused on the things of Christ and not let our minds wander places that it shouldn't. Satan has a way of fooling us into thinking something isn't that bad, or one time isn't going to hurt anything. As Christians we have to keep our minds on the things of God and not of this world all the time, as hard as that can be sometimes. We have to remember this life is a journey and, as the apostle Paul said, we have to stay focused on the road ahead and look forward to the finish line, where our savior will be waiting to greet us. It will be worth it all in the end.

PATIENCE AND WAITING ON THE LORD

Have you not known?

Have you not heard?

The everlasting God, the Lord,

The Creator of the ends of the earth,

Neither faints nor is weary.

His understanding is unsearchable.

He gives power to the weak,

And to those who have no might He increases strength.

Even the youths shall faint and be weary,

And the young men shall utterly fall,

But those who wait on the Lord

Shall renew their strength;

They shall mount up with wings like eagles,

They shall run and not be weary,

They shall walk and not faint.

Isaiah 40:28–31 NKJV

Isaiah 40:31 is one of my favorite verses in the Bible, because it states that, if we wait on the Lord, He will give us the strength and energy to do what He would have us do.

The key words in this passage are, "those who wait on the Lord."

Waiting on anything is not something that most people are good at. We live in a society today where everything is at our fingertips. If we want something, we can do a Google search on the internet and find it. If we are hungry, there are plenty of restaurants to choose from. How many of you love waiting in traffic? Do you say thank you Lord for all the other people on the road today?! Do you think, I'm sure everybody else needs to be somewhere more than I do. Waiting on somebody to tell us what to do and how to do it just isn't in our nature. But yet that is what the Bible tells us we should be doing. When was the last time you prayed and fasted, seeking an answer from God about what you should do? Most people talk to friends and relatives and business associates, but they don't talk to God. There is something about being patient and waiting on God to give us the answer that gives us a sense of assurance and peace of mind, knowing that when we do hear from God, it is always going to be the right answer.

There is a saying that goes "The Lord is never late, He is never early, He is always right on time." I believe the Lord does that to teach us patience and to pray fervently and seek His will about whatever we are praying about. Sometimes, when after a while we don't get an answer from God, that *is* the answer, and it is His way of telling us no.

There are plenty of examples in the Bible about waiting on the Lord.

Jesus himself was thirty years old before He began his ministry, because His Heavenly Father was preparing Him for what He was to face.

When Mary and Martha's brother Lazarus died, the sisters waited frantically on Jesus to show up. When he finally did, Mary scolded him for being so late. Jesus very calmly called Lazarus to come out of the tomb and brought him back to life. I would say that was worth the wait!

When Moses was banished from the Kingdom for beating up a soldier who was beating a Jewish slave, it was forty years before God called on him to lead the Children of Israel to the promised land.

There is something about waiting on the Lord that teaches us patience, and we know when we do get an answer it will be the right answer. I have found that patience comes with age and maybe it is because getting mad and impatient doesn't get us anywhere. If you are waiting on the Lord for an answer, just be patient; He will answer you at just the right time. He always does.

PRAISE HIS HOLY NAME

Sometimes I get really busy with work and forget about God. But God is not to be ignored,. Suddenly a gospel tune comes into my mind and I become more calm, less busy, and let the Holy Spirit minister to me. Our minds all wander once in a while and sometimes will take us to a very dark place. When this happens, remember to do the following:

> *Let all that I am praise the Lord;*
> *with my whole heart, I will praise his holy name.*
> *Let all that I am praise the Lord;*
> *may I never forget the good things he does.*
>
> Psalm 103:1–2 NLT

Whether it is through prayer or music, it will do your soul good just to praise the name of Jesus. In this season of life, I am not able to go to church because of illness, but sometimes I will just put on music and have church by myself and the Holy Spirit.

Take time to praise God in your own way today.

PRAISE THE LORD IN ALL THINGS

I will bless the Lord at all times;
His praise shall continually be in my mouth.
My soul shall make its boast in the Lord;
The humble shall hear of it and be glad.
Oh, magnify the Lord with me,
And let us exalt His name together.

Psalm 34:1–3 NKJV

Praising God daily is an essential part of our walk with Jesus. We have a tendency to tell the Lord what we want and complain about how things are going in our life. How much time do you spend thanking Him and praising Him for all the things He has done for you? Whenever someone helps you out with something you can't do yourself, you wouldn't think twice about saying, "Thank you." It is the same way with God: He loves it when we praise Him and thank Him for all He done in our lives—maybe things that wouldn't have happened without His help. We should praise God in every area of our life. Whether it is good or bad doesn't matter; God loves you and would never do anything to harm you. If there are bad things happening in your life, it isn't God causing those things to happen. Satan is alive and well and creating havoc anywhere he can. Whenever you blame God for something Satan did, Satan loves it because he will do anything to create a rift between you and God. That is why you should Praise God for all things, every day. Satan cannot stay where the name of Jesus is spoken.

So, give Him all the praise and all the glory every day. He is your Savior and your Protector.

Praise God!

We give you praise today, Lord, for all the wonderful things you have done, and what you are continuing to do. Let us give you praise, for Holy is your Name.

PRAY ABOUT EVERYTHING

> *Rejoice in the Lord always. I will say it again: Rejoice! Let your gentleness be evident to all. The Lord is near. Do not be anxious about anything, but in everything, by prayer and petition, with thanksgiving, present your requests to God. And the peace of God, which transcends all understanding, will guard your hearts and your minds in Christ Jesus.*
>
> Philippians 4:4–7 NIV84

Paul can't emphasize enough the importance of rejoicing in the Lord in all circumstances. It is a theme that he has sounded throughout the book of Philippians and is one that is worth repeating, because it is sometimes difficult to give thanks and praise to God when we are going through a tough time in our lives. Paul gives us a blueprint on how to do exactly that: he says we are to pray about everything! When we are not praying, that is when Satan starts attacking and putting doubts in our mind. Prayer is the number one key to fighting off depression and self-doubt. It is through prayer we get the strength to keep on going in spite of our circumstances. If we talk to God about everything that is going on in our lives, we will have a peace about everything.

PRAYER AND FAITH

God answers prayer, and it doesn't matter who you are. The key is to have faith and believe God will answer that prayer. God knows what you need before you ask, and he will supply all of your needs according to his riches in glory (Philippians 4:19). That doesn't mean every prayer is going to be answered. God answers prayers that he knows are sincere and will ultimately glorify him. Prayer without faith is like trying unlock a door without a key.

> *Is any one of you in trouble? He should pray. Is anyone happy? Let him sing songs of praise. Is any one of you sick? He should call the elders of the church to pray over him and anoint him with oil in the name of the Lord. And the prayer offered in faith will make the sick person well; the Lord will raise him up. If he has sinned, he will be forgiven. Therefore confess your sins to each other and pray for each other so that you may be healed. The prayer of a righteous man is powerful and effective.*
>
> James 5:13–16 NIV84

Just believing that God exists is one thing, but having the faith to believe He will answer prayer is something else. Even people who are not saved believe in God. You have to believe that God is your savior and really believe he answers prayer.

Is your faith strong enough to believe He will answer your prayers?

> *But without faith it is impossible to please him: for he that cometh to God must believe that he is, and that he is a rewarder of them that diligently seek him.*

Hebrews 11:6 KJV

PRAYER IS ESSENTIAL

What causes fights and quarrels among you? Don't they come from your desires that battle within you? You want something but don't get it. You kill and covet, but you cannot have what you want. You quarrel and fight. You do not have, because you do not ask God. When you ask, you do not receive, because you ask with wrong motives, that you may spend what you get on your pleasures.

You adulterous people, don't you know that friendship with the world is hatred toward God? Anyone who chooses to be a friend of the world becomes an enemy of God. Or do you think Scripture says without reason that the spirit he caused to live in us envies intensely? But he gives us more grace. That is why Scripture says, "God opposes the proud but gives grace to the humble."

Submit yourselves, then, to God. Resist the devil, and he will flee from you. Come near to God and he will come near to you. Wash your hands, you sinners, and purify your hearts, you double-minded. Grieve, mourn and wail. Change your laughter to mourning and your joy to gloom. Humble yourselves before the Lord, and he will lift you up.

James 4:1–10 NIV 84

This is one of the most compelling passages on prayer and how to pray. James says we pray for the wrong motives and argue with each other about what to pray about. Satan has a way of making us pray for things that God would never approve of, and we pray very selfish prayers. We must humble ourselves before God and make sure that what we pray for will glorify God. Most importantly, we must resist the devil and he will flee if speak the name of Jesus, because Satan cannot be where the name of Jesus is spoken. It is pretty easy to tell if Satan is putting ideas in your head: Just ask yourself if what you are praying about will glorify God—or yourself. God wants to answer our prayers and give us good things, but they have to be something that will also give God the glory.

PRAYING AND FAITH

Is any one of you in trouble? He should pray. Is anyone happy? Let him sing songs of praise. Is any one of you sick? He should call the elders of the church to pray over him and anoint him with oil in the name of the Lord. And the prayer offered in faith will make the sick person well; the Lord will raise him up. If he has sinned, he will be forgiven. Therefore confess your sins to each other and pray for each other so that you may be healed. The prayer of a righteous man is powerful and effective.

Elijah was a man just like us. He prayed earnestly that it would not rain, and it did not rain on the land for three and a half years. Again he prayed, and the heavens gave rain, and the earth produced its crops.

James 5:13–18 NIV84

God answers prayer—and it doesn't matter who you are. The key is to have faith and believe God will answer that prayer. God knows what you need before you ask, and He will supply all of your needs according to His riches in glory. That doesn't mean every prayer is going to be answered. God answers prayers that He knows are sincere and are about something you need, and that will ultimately glorify Him. So, when you pray for a new 4-wheel-drive extended cab super heavy duty truck, you have to figure out how *that* will glorify God! Maybe you can use it to bring kids to church!

Are you praying with faith, or are you just talking out loud? Do you really believe God will answer you when you pray? Remember, it takes faith with prayer every time you bow your head. You might be amazed by the results!

I have heard people say, "I just threw up a prayer." Prayer to God isn't magic that produces instant results. "Just throwing up a prayer" doesn't sound very sincere. Praying a prayer out of desperation and genuinely needing God's help—that is a prayer that God will listen to. It is a mystery why some prayers are answered, and some are not. Only God knows the answers to that question. Only God knows what the future holds, and whether a prayer will help you or hurt you. He is always going to do what is best for you and what you need.

PRAYING FOR THE SICK

Is any one of you in trouble? He should pray. Is anyone happy? Let him sing songs of praise. Is any one of you sick? He should call the elders of the church to pray over him and anoint him with oil in the name of the Lord. And the prayer offered in faith will make the sick person well; the Lord will raise him up. If he has sinned, he will be forgiven. Therefore confess your sins to each other and pray for each other so that you may be healed. The prayer of a righteous man is powerful and effective.

Elijah was a man just like us. He prayed earnestly that it would not rain, and it did not rain on the land for three and a half years. Again he prayed, and the heavens gave rain, and the earth produced its crops.

My brothers, if one of you should wander from the truth and someone should bring him back, remember this: Whoever turns a sinner from the error of his way will save him from death and cover over a multitude of sins.

James 5:13–20 NIV 84

The prayer of a righteous man is powerful and effective. We need righteous men and women to pray for the needs of the church every single day. It is very important that we live our lives in such a way that we are able to pray for others needs and for their salvation. If we are not living a godly life ourselves, we become a stumbling block to others. We cannot be sinning and praying for others' sins at the same time. That is why it is so important for us to purify ourselves and be ready to pray for others. God cannot look upon sin and we cannot be effective in serving God if we are sinning and not keeping ourselves pure and avoiding sin.

PULLING DOWN STRONGHOLDS

> *For though we walk in the flesh, we do not war according to the flesh. For the weapons of our warfare are not carnal but mighty in God for pulling down strongholds, casting down arguments and every high thing that exalts itself against the knowledge of God, bringing every thought into captivity to the obedience of Christ, and being ready to punish all disobedience when your obedience is fulfilled.*
>
> 2 Corinthians 10:3–5 NKJV

We all have things that we struggle with, and we fight to conquer those things. Satan knows all of our weaknesses and that is where he will attack us and try to wear us down, so we give in. That is why every day we have to pray that God will give us the strength to fight against those things. Satan will try to convince you that you are not really following Christ, and that you are a sinner. The very reason he is tempting you is because you are one of Christ's children and he would like nothing more than to see you fail. If you really weren't following Christ, Satan would leave you alone because he would have won.

Give it all to Jesus every day and He will fight those battles for you, and you will have the victory, because Satan cannot dwell where the name of Christ is spoken and those strongholds will be torn down. Blessings to you as go through each day praising God as you do.

PURE HEARTS

> *Create in me a pure heart, O God,*
> *and renew a steadfast spirit within me.*
> *Do not cast me from your presence*
> *or take your Holy Spirit from me.*
> *Restore to me the joy of your salvation*
> *and grant me a willing spirit, to sustain me.*
>
> Psalm 51:10–12 NIV

The author of this Psalm is fervently asking God to renew his relationship with God and to give him the joy that he once had. We all, at one time or another, have had to ask God for forgiveness and restore us to the place we once were in our relationship with Him. We all desire a pure heart, but sometimes that can be very difficult to do in the world we live in. There is temptation all around us and it is vital that we sustain our relationship with Him and receive the joy that the Lord gives us. The Joy of the Lord is very special, there is nothing like it.

PURSUING PEACE

> *Turn from evil and do good;*
> *seek peace and pursue it.*
>
> Psalm 34:14 NIV

What we have to remember and rely on is that Christ said He would give us peace; a peace that passes all understanding.

> *Rejoice in the Lord always. Again I will say, rejoice! Let your gentleness be known to all men. The Lord is at hand. Be anxious for nothing, but in everything by prayer and supplication, with thanksgiving, let your requests be made known to God; and the peace of God, which surpasses all understanding, will guard your hearts and minds through Christ Jesus.*
>
> Philippians 4:4–7 NKJV

And If we have the peace of God in our hearts, then we have nothing to fear. We are His people and He will be there for us, no matter what happens. God can see far into the future and only He knows what is going to happen; we just have to trust and obey.

Sometimes God is all you have, and you have cry out to Him for help when you have tried everything else. His peace is like no other. You will know without a doubt when God has given you peace about what to do.

This is one of the most comforting passages of scripture in the Bible, and verse six is my favorite: Be anxious for nothing and pray, telling God what our problem is. Sometimes your problems are so overwhelming you don't know what to do. We do everything except pray and give the problems over to God. I have done the same thing, trying to solve my problems on my own and not let anyone else know what is really going on (sounds like a typical male doesn't it?). Men tend to be very stubborn and usually wind up making things worse. Peace doesn't come out of a bottle or something you inhale; it only comes from God. Once you receive it, you will never let go because you will discover that God is your rock and you protector.

Truly my soul finds rest in God; my salvation comes from him.
Truly he is my rock and my salvation; he is my fortress, I will never be shaken.

Psalm 62:1–2 NIV

PUTTING YOURSELF IN GOD'S HANDS

Have you ever said, "I am putting it in God's hands, there is nothing I can do." And then you put the problem back in your hands and try to work it out yourself. I know that I have—and made things worse than they were before.

> *Commit your way to the Lord, Trust also in Him, And He shall bring it to pass.*
>
> Psalm 37:5 NKJV

When you were a child, did someone give you something and then want it back? You called them an Indian giver (today that would be politically incorrect). God doesn't work that way. He knows that we all have doubts and fears which will eventually cause us to realize that putting our problems in God's hands was the right thing to do after all. By trusting Him and committing ourselves to follow His will in our life, it will always be the right thing to do. Sometimes it takes a while (and not as quickly as we would like) for it to happen, but it is always the best thing for us, no matter how long it takes.

If you are struggling with something in your life, give it to God. He will always help you do the right thing.

QUIET CHRISTIAN LIFE

> *Now about brotherly love we do not need to write to you, for you yourselves have been taught by God to love each other. And in fact, you do love all the brothers throughout Macedonia. Yet we urge you, brothers, to do so more and more. Make it your ambition to lead a quiet life, to mind your own business and to work with your hands, just as we told you, so that your daily life may win the respect of outsiders and so that you will not be dependent on anybody.*
>
> 1 Thessalonians 4:9–12 NIV84

This is probably one of the most practical passages of scripture in the Bible because it spells out very clearly how we are to conduct ourselves. It tells us to lead a quiet life; we shouldn't go out looking for trouble. We should be worried about taking care of our families and spending time with God instead of constantly complaining about everything under the sun. Some people just can't stand to be quiet. They always have to be talking and complaining. Paul tells us to mind our own business and not be constantly interfering in other people's lives where we are not wanted. There is difference between someone asking for help and assisting them with whatever they need and barging in and taking over. Some people tend to have what I call "Mother Hen Syndrome," where they want to swoop in and solve everyone's problems for them. Your job isn't to solve everyone's problems, but to pray for them and help them find the direction in life they are looking for.

> *The fruit of righteousness will be peace;*
> *the effect of righteousness will be quietness and confidence forever.*
> *My people will live in peaceful dwelling places,*
> *in secure homes,*
> *in undisturbed places of rest.*
>
> Isaiah 32:17–18 NIV84

If we live according to God's will in our lives and spend time in prayer and seeking Him, we will have the confidence we need to make the right decisions in our lives. We will have that security and peace that we all long for because we will know it is right. If you make the right decisions, you will feel good about yourself. But, if make the wrong decisions, you will feel terrible and will beat yourself up over it. We all make wrong decisions and all we have to do is ask forgiveness for them and ask the Holy Spirit to help us make the right decision. Then we will have the peace of knowing it is in God's hands.

RAISING CHILDREN GOD'S WAY

How to raise a child has been a fierce subject of debate over the years. The Bible gives us a lot of insight into how to raise a child who will follow Christ when they become an adult.

> *Train a Child in the way he should go and when he is old he will not turn from it.*
>
> Proverbs 22:7 NIV 84

A lot of us in the boomer generation were raised in church and heard a lot of fire and brimstone sermons about going to hell if we didn't repent right now. I think I was at the altar every Sunday night repenting of the sins I had committed that week. God was portrayed as an angry god who was eager to punish the sinners if they didn't repent.

God was angry at the children of Israel who defied God many times. God left the older generation in the desert and only the younger generation was able to enter the promised land.

Four hundred years later, God sent his son Jesus to earth as a baby to eventually become the Christ. When he began his ministry, he was 30 years old and he taught that God loves his children and if they have sinned, all they had to do was to pray and ask for forgiveness, doing away with the old system of animal sacrifice to atone for sin. Jesus' ministry on earth ended when he died on the cross as a sacrifice for our sins.

So what does all this have to do with raising children? It's really very simple. Go to church as a family and make sure the children are being taught about the Bible. In todays culture, parents send their children to church and don't go themselves. How are you to set an example for them if you stay home and watch the football game? It is vital that parents spend time with their children helping them in reading and understanding the Bible.

There is no doubt we are living in the end times. It is even more critical that families stick together and set the example for your friends and family.

> *For God so loved the world, that he gave his only begotten Son, that whoever*
> *believes in Him should not perish but have everlasting life.*
>
> John 3:16 NKJV

REAR GUARD

The Lord will go before you. The God of Israel will be your rear guard. Looking back at the past year, it is always a mixture of good memories and some sad memories. That is what life is, a lot of memories; some regrets, some triumphs. God is the god of yesterday, today, and tomorrow. Some of you may have regrets about things that happened this year, but God uses those things to help us grow and do better in the future. We should never be satisfied with our past.

It is not our accomplishments, but rather always looking forward to what God has for us. That is the goal of every Christian. People who sit and dwell on the glory days of the past are rotting away in their own memories rather than making new ones. There is a difference between remembering the past and living there. You may not be able to do all of the things you once could, but as long as you are still breathing, you can do something. Notice what this scripture says:

> *But you will not leave in haste or go in flight; for the Lord will go before you, and the God of Israel will be your rear guard.*
>
> Isaiah 52:12 NIV

That means He is not going to let the past prevent you from doing the will of God in the future. Some people tend to dwell on the mistakes of the past and let Satan convince them they are no good to God. God forgives our past and gives us a future to look forward to with excitement. If we don't adopt the attitude of "CAN'T WAIT TO SEE WHAT GOD IS GOING TO DO NEXT IN YOUR LIFE," personally and as a church; if we are not looking forward and seeking God, waiting on the Lord to lead us into the future, then we are going backwards. I've heard it said, "we can't afford to just be normal and skating through life waiting to go to heaven, there is no retirement from serving God." If you think just because you are a Christian, Satan has retired and is not after your soul, you are sadly mistaken. People who just skate along, thinking their salvation is secure, are going to be in for a big surprise someday.

> *I know your deeds, that you are neither cold nor hot. I wish you were either one or the other! So, because you are lukewarm — neither hot nor cold—I am about to spit you out of my mouth.*
>
> Revelation 3:15-16 NIV

If you are hot, you are alive and looking for ways to serve the Lord. If you are cold, you have quit and are just waiting on the Lord to come get them. I have heard people say "I just want to die and go be with Jesus." You are going to die someday and go be with Jesus, but in the meantime he expects you to be doing everything you can and using your gifts to be of service to Him. Inviting someone to church doesn't require a lot of effort, praying with someone is something everyone can do. You don't have to preach, teach or play a musical instrument to be of service to God. I don't believe that is too much to ask! Prayer changes things; prayer moves mountains and heals the sick. Prayer makes the difference between being hot, cold or lukewarm.

GOD WILL GO BEFORE US AND HE WILL BE OUR REAR GUARD

> *The prayer of a righteous man is powerful and effective.*
>
> James 5:16 NIV

223

REFUGE

> *Whoever dwells in the shelter of the Most High*
> *will rest in the shadow of the Almighty.*
> *I will say of the Lord, "He is my refuge and my fortress,*
> *my God, in whom I trust."*
>
> Psalm 91:1–2 NIV

Have you ever been caught out in a really bad storm or were in a vehicle and had to wait until the storm passed by before you could continue on your way?

Do you remember what it felt like to finally get to safety and perhaps put on dry clothes?

God is our protector and our shelter in those times when we just have to wait out the storm, because there is nothing else we can do. Knowing that we are under God's protection no matter what the circumstances is a very comforting thought during those storms in our lives, when we don't have anywhere else to go but to Him. If you are going through a storm right now and you don't know where to go, just remember God is there with you until the storm passes by.

RESTORATION

Brothers, if someone is caught in a sin, you who are spiritual should restore him gently. But watch yourself, or you also may be tempted. Carry each other's burdens, and in this way you will fulfill the law of Christ. If anyone thinks he is something when he is nothing, he deceives himself. Each one should test his own actions. Then he can take pride in himself, without comparing himself to somebody else, for each one should carry his own load.

Anyone who receives instruction in the word must share all good things with his instructor.

Do not be deceived: God cannot be mocked. A man reaps what he sows. The one who sows to please his sinful nature, from that nature will reap destruction; the one who sows to please the Spirit, from the Spirit will reap eternal life. Let us not become weary in doing good, for at the proper time we will reap a harvest if we do not give up. Therefore, as we have opportunity, let us do good to all people, especially to those who belong to the family of believers.

Galatians 6:1–10 NIV

It is our job as believers to help those who stumble and fall back into sin: To help them find forgiveness and to help them get back into a right relationship with Jesus Christ. All too often in the church we tend to be very judgmental towards those who fall—and we tend to forget that we all have sinned. People who are trying to find forgiveness and restoration need a lot of prayer and support from the church, to be able to find the strength to go on, and to be able to forgive themselves. That is what carrying each other's burdens means: Standing with someone through the trials in their life; not abandoning them and judging them for their failures. There used to be a bumper sticker that read, "Christians are not perfect just forgiven." Sometimes we forget that it is not our job to judge others; it is our job to love them and help bring them back into a right relationship with Jesus Christ.

RESTORATION, REAPING AND SOWING

> *Brothers and sisters, if someone is caught in a sin, you who live by the Spirit should restore that person gently. But watch yourselves, or you also may be tempted. Carry each other's burdens, and in this way you will fulfill the law of Christ. If anyone thinks they are something when they are not, they deceive themselves. Each one should test their own actions. Then they can take pride in themselves alone, without comparing themselves to someone else, for each one should carry their own load. Nevertheless, the one who receives instruction in the word should share all good things with their instructor. Do not be deceived: God cannot be mocked. A man reaps what he sows. Whoever sows to please their flesh, from the flesh will reap destruction; whoever sows to please the Spirit, from the Spirit will reap eternal life. Let us not become weary in doing good, for at the proper time we will reap a harvest if we do not give up. Therefore, as we have opportunity, let us do good to all people, especially to those who belong to the family of believers.*
>
> Galatians 6:1–10 NIV

It is our job as a church to help those who stumble and fall back into sin to find forgiveness, and to help them get back into a right relationship with Jesus Christ. All too often we in the church tend to be very judgmental towards those people, and forget that we have all sinned and fallen short of the glory of God. People who are going through temptations and are trying to find forgiveness and restoration need a lot of prayer and support from the church to find the strength to go on, and to be able to forgive themselves; that is what carrying each other's burdens means. Standing with someone through the trials in their life, not abandoning them, and not judging them for their failures. There is a bumper sticker that reads "Christians are not perfect, just forgiven," and sometimes we forget that it is not our job to judge others. It is our job to love them and help bring them back into the right relationship with Jesus Christ.

> But Jesus went to the Mount of Olives. At dawn he appeared again in the temple courts, where all the people gathered around him, and he sat down to teach them. The teachers of the law and the Pharisees brought in a woman caught in adultery. They made her stand before the group and said to Jesus, "Teacher, this woman was caught in the act of adultery. In the Law Moses commanded us to stone such women. Now what do you say?" They were using this question as a trap, in order to have a basis for accusing him. But Jesus bent down and started to write on the ground with his finger. When they kept on questioning him, he straightened up and said to them, "Let any one of you who is without sin be the first to throw a stone at her." Again he stooped down and wrote on the ground. At this, those who heard began to go away one at a time, the older ones first, until only Jesus was left, with the woman still standing there. Jesus straightened up and asked her, "Woman, where are they? Has no one condemned you?" "No one, sir," she said. "Then neither do I condemn you," Jesus declared. "Go now and leave your life of sin."

John 8:1–11 NIV

Jesus told the woman she was forgiven, and he would not condemn her. He told her to leave her life of sin, saying the hardest part for her wasn't being forgiven by Jesus—that was the easy part. The hard part was forgiving herself in the judgment and condemnation of other people. It is our job as a church to help people like this woman know that they are forgiven; neither Christ, nor anybody else is going to condemn them for it. Now this woman still had to live with the consequences she brought upon herself. She had reaped what she had sown. She still had to live with the consequences of committing adultery and the shame and the damage she had done to her family. We all live with the consequences of our sin and the damage that sin causes in our lives. Divorce is a big problem in the church, and it causes heartache to families that are felt for years to come. Drugs and alcohol can cause irreparable physical damage to the body and the consequences are something that people live with the rest of their lives. But that doesn't mean they are not forgiven and they can't start over and have a new life in Christ.

Therefore, there is now no condemnation for those who are in Christ Jesus.

Romans 8:1 NIV

SEEK HIM FIRST

> *And without faith it is impossible to please God, because anyone who comes to him must believe that he exists and that he rewards those who earnestly seek him.*
>
> Hebrews 11:6 NIV

Do you believe He exists? His resurrection is our only hope of our having eternal life. If it isn't true, God help us. I choose to believe that someday, I will get to see the risen savior face to face—how about you?

Robert Lowry wrote these immortal words in *Christ Arose*:

Death cannot keep his prey, Jesus my Savior!
He tore the bars away, Jesus, my Lord!
And up from the grave He arose,
With a mighty triumph o'er His foes.
He arose a victor from the dark domain,
And He lives forever with His saints to reign,
He arose, He arose, Hallelujah! Christ Arose!

Reverend Billy Graham said this about the Bible and Jesus:

If I didn't believe that the Bible and the Gospel of Jesus Christ held the answer to this world's baffling problems, I would go back to the farm and the rural life that I love and spend my days in peaceful solitude.[1]

Every morning when you get up and look at the risen sun, remember to think about the risen Son and give Him thanks for what He did on that cross for you.

Even the sun is going to go away someday. The Bible tells us that we will have no need of the sun, the moon, or the stars, because the light of the glory of the Son of God will be all the light we need. Worship the Son today and every day.

---

1. Billy Graham, *The Hour of Decision,* January 9th, 1955

SELFLESS SERVICE

On one occasion an expert in the law stood up to test Jesus. "Teacher," he asked, "what must I do to inherit eternal life?"

"What is written in the Law?" he replied. "How do you read it?"

He answered: "'Love the Lord your God with all your heart and with all your soul and with all your strength and with all your mind'; and, 'Love your neighbor as yourself.'"

"You have answered correctly," Jesus replied. "Do this and you will live."

But he wanted to justify himself, so he asked Jesus, "And who is my neighbor?"

In reply Jesus said: "A man was going down from Jerusalem to Jericho, when he fell into the hands of robbers. They stripped him of his clothes, beat him and went away, leaving him half dead. A priest happened to be going down the same road, and when he saw the man, he passed by on the other side. So too, a Levite, when he came to the place and saw him, passed by on the other side. But a Samaritan, as he traveled, came where the man was; and when he saw him, he took pity on him. He went to him and bandaged his wounds, pouring on oil and wine. Then he put the man on his own donkey, took him to an inn and took care of him. The next day he took out two silver coins and gave them to the innkeeper. 'Look after him,' he said, 'and when I return, I

will reimburse you for any extra expense you may have.'
Which of these three do you think was a neighbor to the man who fell into
the hands of robbers?"
The expert in the law replied, "The one who had mercy on him." Jesus told
him, "Go and do likewise."

Luke 10:25–37 NIV84

A lot of us tend to be like the priest and the Levite in this story. We don't want to get involved; we have enough trouble of our own without getting involved with other people's problems. But, that isn't what Jesus tells us to do, is it? He commands us to get involved and help others.

Whenever you reach out to help someone else, you are pleasing God, doing what is right in the Kingdom of Heaven and here on earth.

The harvest is plentiful but the workers are few. Ask the Lord of the harvest,
therefore, to send out workers into his harvest field.

Matthew 9:37–38 NIV

Jesus taught that we are to share our faith with others, along with doing what we can to help our fellow man. He didn't say, go to church every Sunday and you will enter the kingdom of heaven. "And if anyone gives even a cup of cold water to one of these little ones because he is my disciple, I tell you the truth, he will certainly not lose his reward" (Matthew 10:42, NIV).

SERVING THE LORD WITH GLADNESS

> *And whatever you do, do it heartily, as to the Lord and not to men, knowing that from the Lord you will receive the reward of the inheritance; for you serve the Lord Christ.*
>
> Colossians 3:23–24 NKJV

Have you ever had a job where you just couldn't get out of bed in the morning and go to work? You basically work there for the paycheck and that's it.

I know I have, and I was absolutely miserable.

The Lord wants you to work for Him with joy, doing the best you can. Work for the Lord should be something that you do because you love it—because you love the Lord—and you should serve the Lord with gladness. It doesn't matter what you are doing, whatever it is, you should do it with an attitude of joy.

Having joy and gladness in your heart by serving Our Lord and Savior will spill over into the rest of your life. People will realize that you seem to have a better attitude at work because you have a smile on your face and a spring in your step. My favorite saying, one I say often from the pulpit is, "There should be no such thing as a grumpy Christian." If you are feeling grumpy and in a bad mood all the time, you should pray about why you are constantly in a bad mood and ask the Lord to help you find out why. Start living the joyful life that you have inside, because you know you have the comforter (The Holy Spirit) with you all the time. The joy of the Lord is something you should have—no matter what your circumstances. Just remember, "The Joy of the Lord is your Strength."

> *For the Lord your God will bless you in all your harvest and in all the work of your hands, and your joy will be complete.*
>
> Deuteronomy 16:15 NIV

SHAKING MOUNTAINS

> *"Though the mountains be shaken and the hills be removed, yet my unfailing love for you will not be shaken nor my covenant of peace be removed," says the Lord, who has compassion on you.*
>
> Isaiah 54:10 NIV

Sometimes in the storms of life, we tend to lose sight of the fact that God's unfailing love is always with us. When we are going through hard times, like trying to figure out how to pay the bills, or deal with a serious illness, we let ourselves get depressed and start trying to rely on our own strength. We tend to forget that no matter what is going on, God is going to be there for us even when the earth is shaking under our feet. Probably the biggest problem most people have is that they get discouraged and they turn to other people and other things for relief. People even turn to alcohol and try to forget about their problems for a while, but guess what? The problems are still there when they get sober.

Come, all you who are thirsty,
come to the waters;
and you who have no money,

come, buy and eat!
Come, buy wine and milk
without money and without cost.
Why spend money on what is not bread,
and your labor on what does not satisfy?
Listen, listen to me, and eat what is good,
and your soul will delight in the richest of fare.
Give ear and come to me;
hear me, that your soul may live.
I will make an everlasting covenant with you,
my faithful love promised to David.

Isaiah 55:1–3 NIV84

When it is all said and done, all we have left is our faith in Christ. There is nothing on this earth that will give us permanent satisfaction like knowing that we are safe in the arms of God. God offers us a place where we will never be hungry or thirsty, where we won't need money to buy things, we won't have to work for a living; it will all free to us by the love and the grace of God. After all, our ultimate goal is to live our lives for God and try to please him with what we do in our daily walk with him. That isn't always easy, but with God's help we can do it.

SPIRIT FRESH

> *Do not merely listen to the word, and so deceive yourselves. Do what it says. Anyone who listens to the word but does not do what it says is like a man who looks at his face in a mirror and goes away and immediately forgets what he looks like. But whoever looks intently into the perfect law that gives freedom, and continues to do this, not forgetting what he has heard, but doing it — he will be blessed in what he does.*
>
> James 1:22–25 NIV84

How many times have you left church on Sunday morning, saying, that was a great message this morning! Then you walk out the door and never think about it. This is what James is talking about here: it doesn't do any good to hear a message or read a passage of scripture and say that is exactly what I needed to hear, and not do anything about it. What would you do if you were at work and your boss gave you a performance review, pointing out some things you needed to work on and you didn't do anything to improve your job performance? Your next review would probably be even worse and you could be fired. The same way in our walk with Christ. If we are not continually trying improve our relationship with God, sooner or later we are going to get lazy and just cruise along and say no big deal, my salvation is secure. Or as in the job, no big deal, I am already good at what I do, the boss is just overreacting. Some of you have been Christians for a long time;

some of you were saved before I was even born! Without a push from the Holy Spirit, you would just stay on auto pilot the rest of your days. How many of you have eaten stale bread or drank sour milk? It went bad because it sat too long. The same thing happens to Christians who lose their zeal for serving God. The only way to stay fresh is by continually seeking God and asking him to show you ways that you can serve Him.

Walking with Christ should be an exciting adventure!

STANDING IN THE GAP

> *I looked for someone who might rebuild the wall of righteousness that guards the land. I searched for someone to stand in the gap in the wall so I wouldn't have to destroy the land, but I found no one.*
>
> Ezekiel 22:30 NLT

Now is not the time for complacency! It doesn't matter whether you are 18 or 80, God needs His people to stand in the gap and fight for the religious freedoms in this nation. Just as the Lord destroyed nations in the days of old, we will lose our freedoms and God will remove his protection over the United States of America. Christians need to fast and pray like never before. God is patient, but his patience will not last forever.

In Ezekiel's day, people ignored all the rhetoric about being attacked by their enemies and he could not find anyone to stand guard over the city. We as Christians have to be alert, paying attention to what is going on around us, and not let our enemies catch us sleeping. America is the greatest nation on earth, but it is not invincible, by any means. There are many groups who are infiltrating our government and are advocating the United States become a socialist nation.

The United States was founded on Biblical principles, by Godly men who prayed constantly for the Lord's protection over them as they built this new nation.

The only thing that will save the United States of America is its people getting on their knees and praying God will forgive us of our sins and protect us.

> *If my people, who are called by my name, will humble themselves and pray and seek my face and turn from their wicked ways, then I will hear from heaven, and I will forgive their sin and will heal their land.*
>
> 2 Chronicles 7:14 NIV

STAYING HUMBLE

> *Humble yourselves, therefore, under God's mighty hand, that he may lift you up in due time. Cast all your anxiety on him because he cares for you. Be self-controlled and alert. Your enemy the devil prowls around like a roaring lion looking for someone to devour. Resist him, standing firm in the faith, because you know that your brothers throughout the world are undergoing the same kind of sufferings. And the God of all grace, who called you to his eternal glory in Christ, after you have suffered a little while, will himself restore you and make you strong, firm and steadfast. To him be the power for ever and ever. Amen.*
>
> 1 Peter 5:6–12 NIV 84

It is so important to be constantly aware of our surroundings, and aware of what is going on in our own life. It is so easy to rationalize sin, saying to ourselves that we are not hurting anyone and that what we do in the privacy of our own homes is our own business. But we forget that God knows what we are doing and his Holy Spirit is always with us, gently nudging us to turn from sin and surrender our will to Him.

Everything is permissible for me—but not everything is beneficial. Everything is permissible for me—but I will not be mastered by anything.

1 Corinthians 6:12 NIV84

The following by Charles Swindoll says it better than I can:

No one is completely free from bad habits; it is the price we pay for being human. Habits are as numerous as every detail of life; the list is endless. But let's focus on five suggestions that will help us.

Stop rationalizing: Refuse to make comments like, "Oh, that's just me. I'm just like that, always have been, always will be. After all, nobody's perfect." Such excuses take the edge off disobedience and encourage you to diminish or completely ignore the Spirit's work of conviction.

Apply strategy: Approach your target with a rifle, not a shotgun. Take on each habit one at a time, not all at once. Be realistic: It won't happen fast. It won't be easy. Nor will your resolve be permanent overnight. Periodic failures, however, are still better than habitual slavery. Be encouraged: Realize you're on the road to ultimate triumph, for the first time in years! Enthusiasm strengthens self discipline and prompts an attitude of stick-to-it-iveness.

Start Today: This is the best moment thus far in your life. To put it off is as an admission of defeat and will only intensify and prolong the self confidence battle.

Extracting the painful thorns of habit enables the pilgrim to focus less attention on himself and more attention on the One who is worthy. And the most exciting thought of all is that He will be right there in the morning ready to help you through the day with all the power you will need, one moment at a time.[1]

---

1. Charles R. Swindoll. *Growing Strong in the Seasons of Life,* Grand Rapids, MI: Zondervan, 2007.

STRENGTH THROUGH CHRIST

After Ehud came Shamgar son of Anath, who struck down six hundred Philistines with an oxgoad. He too saved Israel.

Judges 3:31 NIV

Shamgar is only mentioned once in the Bible, in one short powerful sentence. One man, one oxgoad, six hundred Philistines! Do you think he did that all on his own? Do you think that maybe God was with him? An oxgoad was a long pole with a sharp end on it to goad animals into moving, but it also was a very powerful weapon in the hand of Shamgar. You think that your problems are too much for God to handle? If so, then your God is too small, but my God can handle anything this world can throw at me and He always wins. It is amazing how God can use the smallest things under the most difficult circumstances to show us that he is still on the throne of heaven and in charge of this world.

But God chose the foolish things of the world to shame the wise; God chose the weak things of the world to shame the strong. He chose the lowly things of this world and the despised things—and the things that are not—to nullify the things that are, so that no one may boast before him. It is because of him that

244

you are in Christ Jesus, who has become for us wisdom from God—that is, our righteousness, holiness and redemption. Therefore, as it is written: "Let him who boasts boast in the Lord."

1 Corinthians 1:27–31 NIV84

God could have sent a thousand men out to help Shamgar slay those six hundred Philistines, but he didn't. Then God would not have gotten the glory. One thousand against six hundred would have been pretty good odds.

One man against six hundred however, that is just plain suicide. There is no way Shamgar could have done it without God—and God gets the glory. Through Shamgar, God showed the children of Israel that if they would obey Him and follow His commandments, He would go before them and defeat their enemies. This happened during a period of time after the death of Moses and Joshua and their generation. The next generation had not seen or lived through all of the things that God had done in delivering their enemies into their hands. This younger generation had turned from God and were worshipping idols and intermarrying with the people that had been captured during the time of Joshua.

God needed them to understand that He was still in charge, and He could help them get out of trouble and rescue them, just as He did with Moses and Joshua.

That is why it is so important to remember the lessons that history has taught us, and the things that He brought our ancestors through to obtain victory. God is still just as capable of doing miracles today as he was back in the day of Moses and Joshua.

Stay focused on God and He will see you through whatever seemingly unsurmountable problems you have today.

SUCCESS—WHAT IS IT?

> *As I was with Moses, so I will be with you; I will never leave you nor forsake you. Be strong and courageous, because you will lead these people to inherit the land I swore to their ancestors to give them. Be strong and very courageous. Be careful to obey all the law my servant Moses gave you; do not turn from it to the right or to the left, that you may be successful wherever you go. Keep this Book of the Law always on your lips; meditate on it day and night, so that you may be careful to do everything written in it. Then you will be prosperous and successful.*
>
> Joshua 1:5b–8

Success is something that everyone wants, but not everyone achieves it.

To be really successful, you have to set a goal that is realistic to achieve. Anything worth working for is worth the effort to get there. It doesn't matter what you choose to do, as long as your are good at it and you enjoy it. There is nothing worse than going to work every day to a job you hate. Some people work two or three jobs just to make ends meet. That doesn't sound very goal oriented to me—unless your goal is an early grave. Decide what you want and focus on that one goal with everything you have.

I worked a few jobs that I didn't like doing, and I have even worked two jobs because I had to. But it paid the bills until I found something better. Nobody ever starts out being in charge; you have to prove you are willing to work hard and be trusted with more responsibility.

When Moses died, the Lord chose Joshua to replace Moses and lead the Children of Israel into the promised land. He gave Joshua some very specific instruction on how to be successful in his mission to be the new leader of the Children of Israel.

They were really very simple rules. They told Joshua he was to obey God and always keep the book of the law with him all the time. Those books of the law are what we call the first five books of the Bible today. The Lord gave Joshua the courage, wisdom, and strength to be successful. You can do the same thing today by reading God's word and listening to what God is telling you to do. It's hard to do what you are told if you are not listening to what you are being told! Joshua listened and he was very successful. You can be too.

SUDDEN DEATH

Death isn't a subject that people like to talk about, or even think about. But it will happen to all of us eventually, whether we like it or not. Thanks to Jesus' death and resurrection, life after death will be the most wonderful thing that you will ever experience.

> *Come now, you who say, "Today or tomorrow we will go to such and such a city, spend a year there, buy and sell, and make a profit"; whereas you do not know what will happen tomorrow. For what is your life? It is even a vapor that appears for a little time and then vanishes away. Instead you ought to say, "If the Lord wills, we shall live and do this or that." But now you boast in your arrogance. All such boasting is evil.*
>
> James 4:13–16 NKJV

Sudden death is a term that is used often in sports. When the score is tied, the first team to score wins. Sudden death is also something that happens in life! We all have known or heard about people who have died unexpectedly.

When someone dies suddenly, it is always a tragedy, but the bigger tragedy is if they die not knowing the Lord—that is a real tragedy. If someone dies and knows the Lord, their death is always very sad, but knowing they are in heaven eases the grief, because we know they are in a better place. If they die and have not accepted Jesus Christ as their personal savior, it is a real tragedy. Just like some deaths, it is preventable. Accepting Jesus as your savior is a very simple process and one that will ease your mind knowing that, if you die suddenly, you are going be in heaven.

In the above scripture James tells us not to boast about tomorrow because it may never come. We all make plans about the future, but James is telling us to also be prepared. Live your life as if you are going to live forever, but be prepared if tomorrow never arrives for you.

SUFFERING

The Lord God took the man and put him in the Garden of Eden to work it and take care of it. And the Lord God commanded the man, "You are free to eat from any tree in the garden; but you must not eat from the tree of the knowledge of good and evil, for when you eat from it you will certainly die."

The Lord God said, "It is not good for the man to be alone. I will make a helper suitable for him."

Now the Lord God had formed out of the ground all the wild animals and all the birds in the sky. He brought them to the man to see what he would name them; and whatever the man called each living creature, that was its name. So the man gave names to all the livestock, the birds in the sky and all the wild animals.

But for Adam no suitable helper was found. So the Lord God caused the man to fall into a deep sleep; and while he was sleeping, he took one of the man's ribs and then closed up the place with flesh. Then the Lord God made a woman from the rib he had taken out of the man, and he brought her to the man.

Genesis 2:15–22 NIV

In order to understand why God lets people suffer, we have to go back to the Garden of Eden and the sins that Adam and Eve committed. When God put them in the Garden, it was to be caretakers of the Garden and all the creatures that lived there. They had an abundance of fruit and vegetables to choose from and there was only one tree that God told them not to touch: The tree of knowledge of good and evil. Up to this point they did not have the ability to know right from wrong. They were obedient to God and did as they were told.

God's nemesis Satan snuck into the Garden as a serpent that we assume was a snake and all the creatures could talk to each other at that time. Satan smooth-talked Eve into eating from the forbidden tree and, as soon as she did, she gave a bit to Adam. They immediately realized they were naked and had sinned by eating from the forbidden tree. To make a long story short, they were kicked out of the garden and forced to make a living on their own and became farmers, planting crops in order to survive,

From that point on, everyone who was born reached a point when they were old enough to be punished for their sins. Their bodies would feel pain when they got hurt and, as they grew older, they would feel a lot of pain as their bodies wore out and they died.

So, sin, pain, and suffering are a part of our lives and, just like Adam and Eve, we do things that are wrong because we are curious and fall into the trap called Sin.

Satan is very good at making evil things look very attractive and, just like Eve, we fall for his old tricks.

The only defense we have against Satan is accepting Jesus Christ as our savior and ask His protection from sin and the ability to fight the devil. We can't do it alone; that is why the Holy Spirit is with us to ward off enemy attacks.

Adam and Eve failed the test of temptation in the Garden of Eden, and we have been paying the price ever since.

Aren't you glad God loved us enough to provide forgiveness of sin and protection of the Holy Spirit?

SUFFERING DOESN'T LAST FOREVER

> *He was despised and rejected by mankind, a man of suffering, and familiar with pain. Like one from whom people hide their faces he was despised, and we held him in low esteem. Surely he took up our pain and bore our suffering, yet we considered him punished by God, stricken by him, and afflicted. But he was pierced for our transgressions, he was crushed for our iniquities; the punishment that brought us peace was on him, and by his wounds we are healed. We all, like sheep, have gone astray, each of us has turned to our own way; and the Lord has laid on him the iniquity of us all. He was oppressed and afflicted, yet he did not open his mouth; he was led like a lamb to the slaughter, and as a sheep before its shearers is silent, so he did not open his mouth. By oppression and judgment he was taken away. Yet who of his generation protested? For he was cut off from the land of the living; for the transgression of my people he was punished.*
>
> Isaiah 53:3–8 NIV

The Savior of the world would be beaten beyond recognition, have a crown of thorns put on his head, hung on a cross, barely even conscious, to die for the sins of the world. He went through some of the most horrible things. Today we can't even imagine how people could treat someone so barbarically. Our capital punishment today is nothing compared to what the Romans were capable of, yet He never said a word in defense of his own actions; He let his actions speak for themselves. All of the things He did spoke volumes about who He was, and I suppose, after that, He knew that if they didn't believe him by then, nothing He could've said would have made a difference. Even today, when God does miraculous things or people are healed, there are those who refuse to believe, and try rationalizing it away as being a freak of nature, or—a popular one—if a person is healed, their disease just went into remission, or was misdiagnosed to begin with. The good news in all of this is that Christ will be victorious in the end.

> *So he will sprinkle many nations, and kings will shut their mouths because of him. For what they were not told, they will see, and what they have not heard, they will understand.*
>
> Isaiah 52:15 NIV

The blood of Jesus was sprinkled on many nations, meaning that salvation was available from that point on to everyone, everywhere. The Jews had rejected him and killed him, but He arose, victorious, to be the Savior of all mankind, not just the Jews. There would be nothing anyone can say; people could no longer deny his deity. All their blasphemy, all their scheming, all their lies would come to naught, because in the end Christ would be victorious. The kings of the earth would shut their mouths and ultimately bow down before him. The second part of this verse is a riddle of sorts: prior to the death and resurrection of Jesus Christ, the gentiles had not heard the gospel, so they couldn't understand.

SUICIDE. ONLY CHRIST HAS THE ANSWER

> *I have seen everything in this meaningless life, including the death of good young people and the long life of wicked people. So don't be too good or too wise! Why destroy yourself? On the other hand, don't be too wicked either. Don't be a fool! Why die before your time? Pay attention to these instructions, for anyone who fears God will avoid both extremes. One wise person is stronger than ten leading citizens of a town! Not a single person on earth is always good and never sins.*
>
> Ecclesiastes 7:15–20 NLT

Suicide is a subject most people do not like to talk about, because it is a very hard subject to even think about. Most people don't know what to say when they hear about someone committing suicide.

I have heard people say, "Why would anyone want to commit suicide?" That is a very rational question. But a person who takes their own life isn't thinking rationally. In their mind, there is no way out of their situation but death. They feel like nobody cares and nothing can help them.

Most people contemplating suicide don't seek counseling because they feel it won't do any good. But there is help available and it starts with Jesus Christ. Giving their life to Christ is the first step to turning their life around. The next step is to find a good Christian counselor who can lead them one step at a time using Biblical references, and help them talk about why they are wanting to end their life. My favorite Bible verse is:

"For I know the plans I have for you," says the Lord. "They are plans for good and not for disaster, to give you a future and a hope. In those days when you pray, I will listen. If you look for me wholeheartedly, you will find me. I will be found by you," says the Lord.

Jeremiah 29:11–14a NLT

This is not something simplistic or easy; it is a daily, lifelong commitment, and requires a willingness to obey Christ and follow Him by praying and reading the Word of God.

I am very familiar with this issue because many years ago, I was lost and not following Christ the way I had most of my life, and I felt suicide was the only way out. Thank God I did not succeed and I rededicated my life to Christ, became an ordained minister and a Hospice Chaplain. This article isn't about me, but I know there are people who will read this who are in the position I was, or know someone who is. Introduce them to Jesus Christ and let Him do the rest. None of us can do anything; but with Christ, all things are possible.

But Jesus looked at them and said to them, "With men this is impossible, but with God all things are possible."

Matthew 19:26 NKJV

TEMPLE OF THE HOLY SPIRIT

> *Don't you know that you yourselves are God's temple and that God's Spirit lives in you?*
> *If anyone destroys God's temple, God will destroy him; for God's temple is sacred, and*
> *you are that temple.*
>
> 1 Corinthians 3:16–17 NIV84

That means you should treat your body with respect and nourish your soul because his Holy Spirit lives and dwells in you. If you trust in Him, you will never be put to shame and He will be with you. Is Jesus Christ the most precious thing in your life? Christianity isn't a religion, it isn't a belief system, it is a way of life. Being able to stay strong in your faith and not stumble is a daily effort. We all have to die daily to self and say yes to the things of God. Like it or not, you are a role model and people watch what you *do* as much as what you *say*. People are looking for examples of how to live a happy and fulfilling life and they are searching for anything that will satisfy them. Just quoting the Bible and passing out tracts on the street corner doesn't work anymore. There is such a loud cacophony of other voices out there trying to reach people for whatever cause they are pushing, that the message of Christ gets drowned out. We have to be the example, modeling a Christian lifestyle so people will know what Christianity is all about. Being a Christian isn't just about going to church and reading the Bible, it is about living a holy life, a life that is pleasing and acceptable to God. Read your Bible and pray; those two actions will reveal what you need to do to live a life acceptable to God.

THANKFUL AND BLESSED

> *Shout for joy to the Lord, all the earth.*
> *Worship the Lord with gladness;*
> *come before him with joyful songs.*
> *Know that the Lord is God.*
> *It is he who made us, and we are his*
> *we are his people, the sheep of his pasture.*
> *Enter his gates with thanksgiving*
> *and his courts with praise;*
> *give thanks to him and praise his name.*
> *For the Lord is good and his love endures forever;*
> *his faithfulness continues through all generations.*
>
> Psalm 100: 1–5 NIV

Lord, we have so much to be thankful for that it is impossible to list everything you have done for us. Most of all, we are thankful for your free gift of salvation and to be able to live in freedom in the United States of America. Just as those people who gave thanks in that first thanksgiving so many years ago, we also thank you for your grace and protection over us as your children.

We here in America have a tendency to take for granted all of the wonderful things we have and have no concept of people living in third world countries who live in shacks and wear rags. They are starving because there is never enough food to go around and, sometimes when there is a drought, water has to be rationed out. We are truly blessed, and it is hard to imagine what a glorious place heaven is going to be, where we sit at the feet of Jesus and worship Him. Where there will be not shortage of food and water.

People of all faiths and all nations will worship the one true God forever and ever.

What a glorious day that will be!

THE COST OF THE CROSS

As they led him away, they seized Simon from Cyrene, who was on his way in from the country, and put the cross on him and made him carry it behind Jesus. A large number of people followed him, including women who mourned and wailed for him. Jesus turned and said to them, "Daughters of Jerusalem, do not weep for me; weep for yourselves and for your children. For the time will come when you will say, 'Blessed are the barren women, the wombs that never bore and the breasts that never nursed!' Then they will say to the mountains, 'Fall on us!' and to the hills, 'Cover us!' For if men do these things when the tree is green, what will happen when it is dry?"

Luke 23:26–32 NIV 84

Have you ever thought about what the cost is of following Jesus Christ? We have all heard the saying, "We all have our cross to bear." The cost of following Jesus Christ doesn't just affect us; it affects people around us, and everything we do. If Jesus dying on the cross would have just affected Him and nobody else, that would have been the end of it. Simon of Cyrene just happened to be in the area and they grabbed him and forced him to carry the cross. Jesus doesn't force anyone to follow Him or to do anything. He calls us to pick up our cross and follow Him. The disciples were the first people His crucifixion affected; it forced them to take a hard look at themselves and why they were following Christ in the first place. Suddenly their world had been turned upside down; their leader had been arrested and was going to be crucified. Every one of them had to decide whether following Jesus Christ was worth the cost that they were going to have to pay. They suddenly realized this was something bigger than themselves—and that is exactly what following Jesus Christ means.

> *Then he said to them all: "If anyone would come after me, he must deny himself and take up his cross daily and follow me. For whoever wants to save his life will lose it, but whoever loses his life for me will save it."*
>
> Luke 9:23–24 NIV 84

When Jesus was crucified what He said took on a whole new meaning. The disciples realized they would have to be willing to die for Christ and be willing to defend His teachings even if meant dying. Taking up your cross means risking alienation of friends and family. It means being willing to be ridiculed for your faith in Christ, and, yes, it means being willing to die for your beliefs. Many hundreds of thousands of people have died through the years defending Christianity, and people are still dying today for the cause of Christ.

THE CROSS AND THE LOST

> *We live by faith, not by sight. We are confident, I say, and would prefer to be away from the body and at home with the Lord. So we make it our goal to please him, whether we are at home in the body or away from it. For we must all appear before the judgment seat of Christ, that each one may receive what is due him for the things done while in the body, whether good or bad.*
>
> 2 Corinthians 5:7–10 NIV84

It isn't the Christians who have to worry, even if we die defending the cause of Christ; we know that we are going to be in heaven with him. It is the non-believers that are going to face the horrible things that Satan is going to bring on this world in the last day. They are the ones who are going to cry out in anguish and want to die to relieve their suffering, because they will not have any relief in sight—and even death won't bring relief to those who don't believe in Jesus Christ. All the people who have died for Christ knew that it would be worth it all; non-believers don't have that assurance. Whenever we decide to follow Christ, we leave everything at the foot of the cross. We leave our pride, our old way of life, our friends and our family, in order to dedicate ourselves to carrying the cross he has called us to bear. Taking up your cross means living by faith. It isn't about asking God to do some great work in us; it is about God being glorified through us. Jesus never brought glory to himself; he always gave glory and honor to the Father. It is only by getting alone with God every day and asking God what we can do to glorify Him that we are truly bearing our cross and following Him. Any success that we have only comes through giving the glory to Him. Taking up your cross means doing your very best to win souls for the lost.

Spurgeon said it best: "If sinners will be damned, at least let them leap to Hell over our bodies. And if they will perish, let them perish with our arms about their knees, imploring them to stay. If Hell must be filled, at least let it be filled in the teeth of our exertions and let not one go there unwarned and un-prayed for."[1]

---

1. C. H. Spurgeon: "The Wailing of Risca" (Metropolitan Tabernacle Sermon No. 349; Delivered on Sabbath Morning, December 9th, 1860, at Exeter Hall, Strand)

THE HAND OF GOD

> *Young men, in the same way be submissive to those who are older. All of you, clothe yourselves with humility toward one another, because, "God opposes the proud but gives grace to the humble." Humble yourselves, therefore, under God's mighty hand, that he may lift you up in due time. Cast all your anxiety on him because he cares for you.*
>
> 1 Peter 5:5–7 NIV84

Have you ever thought about just how powerful is the touch of His Hand? He can perform miracles in your life that you never even dreamed possible. Humble yourself and submit to the power of His Holy Spirit in your life, leaving the life you're living. Why? Because He cares for you. Of all the people in the world, He is concerned about you and what is happening in your life right now, today.

> *When he came down from the mountainside, large crowds followed him. A man with leprosy came and knelt before him and said, "Lord, if you are willing, you can make me clean." Jesus reached out his hand and touched the man. "I am willing," he said. "Be clean!" Immediately he was cured of his leprosy. Then Jesus said to him, "See that you don't tell anyone. But go, show*

yourself to the priest and offer the gift Moses commanded, as a testimony to them."

Matthew 8:1–4 NIV 84

His is the cleansing touch. With a touch of His hand, the man was instantly healed of leprosy. Notice the man asked Jesus if He was willing. Jesus replied He was; his faith led him to go to Jesus and ask him for healing. The bottom line: Jesus is willing to heal you, if you are willing. You can't just say, "I believe God can heal me" you have to act on your faith and say "I believe I am healed. I believe God has cleansed me from sin and is doing a mighty work in my life." I am living proof of that, if I had not had the faith to believe that God healed and gotten up out my power chair and started walking, I would still be in it, but I was healed, because I acted on my faith. Faith plus action equals healing.

THE HEART IS DECEITFUL

> *This is what the Lord says: "Cursed is the one who trusts in man, who draws strength from mere flesh and whose heart turns away from the Lord. That person will be like a bush in the wastelands; they will not see prosperity when it comes. They will dwell in the parched places of the desert, in a salt land where no one lives. But blessed is the one who trusts in the Lord, whose confidence is in him. They will be like a tree planted by the water that sends out its roots by the stream. It does not fear when heat comes; its leaves are always green. It has no worries in a year of drought and never fails to bear fruit." The heart is deceitful above all things and beyond cure. Who can understand it? "I the Lord search the heart and examine the mind, to reward each person according to their conduct, according to what their deeds deserve."*
>
> Jeremiah 17:5–10 NIV

Cursed is the man who trusts in man. That is a very blunt statement about the state of humanity. Jeremiah was saying that if we put our trust in ourselves and other people instead of God, we are doomed to failure before we even start. Have you ever put your trust in someone and gave them your heart, only to have them fail you? How did that feel? You felt betrayed and perhaps so badly hurt that you now have trouble trusting others. Whenever we put our trust in ourselves and others, we are like someone living in the desert with no one around us, and we are left to our own devices to figure out what to do. We can become so bitter and frustrated by our situation that we end up making decisions based on hatred and selfishness, rather than what is best for us. But more importantly, we don't bother to seek God, and ask him to guide us with our lives, and we end up being alone.

Stop trusting in mere humans, who have but a breath in their nostrils. Why hold them in esteem?

Isaiah 2:22 NIV

There are a lot of hurting people in this country because they have put their trust in someone else and have been devastated by deceit and corruption. Many people have put their trust in the stock market, and in some cases lost their life savings. Many people put their trust in investors, and have lost everything because they trusted people to invest their money properly. The Bible calls people like this wolves in sheep's clothing. Many people have put their trust in real estate, and have been ruined financially because of bad investments, and the downturn of the housing market. Many of these people are honest, hard-working, God-fearing people who put their trust in men's wisdom, rather than seeking God before making a decision, doing what seemed right in their own eyes.

Do not be anxious about anything, but in every situation, by prayer and petition, with thanksgiving, present your requests to God. And the peace of God, which transcends all understanding, will guard your hearts and your minds in Christ Jesus.

Philippians 4:6–7 NIV

This is exactly what Jeremiah is talking about in verse six. Blessed is the man who trusts in the Lord. The man whose confidence is in Him. I've personally made a lot of very bad decisions and lost a lot of money in my life because I made those decisions without praying about them first. I wound up being taken advantage of because I trusted in men rather than waiting on God to show me what I should do. We have a tendency to get anxious and impatient. We are afraid if we don't take advantage of an opportunity right now this minute, that it will be gone and we will lose out. Then we look back and realize that if we'd been patient waiting on God for an answer, we wouldn't have wound up in a bad situation that we will be paying on for a long time, financially and emotionally.

Putting our trust in others is like the guy who, on a very windy day, was working on his roof and it had a very sharp peak. So he decided, to be safe, he would secure himself to something on the earth. He tied a rope around his waist, pulled it tight, climbed up on the roof and then over the peak. He threw the rope over the side and said to his boy, tie the rope to that tree. Well, the little kid thought the tree was rather small, so instead he tied it to the bumper of his dad's car. Mom was busy in the house with chores of her own. She discovered that she needed to make a quick trip to the store. She went out, put the car in reverse, and the guy came off the roof a lot faster than he went up. Trusting in the rope is like those who put their trust in others for their security. We need to make sure we can trust that person before we trust them with our lives. The Bible tells us we are to seek godly wisdom. Advice from other Christians can sometimes be helpful, but it isn't a cure to our problem. Only by trusting in God will we get the answer right every time.

THE LORD'S PRAYER EXPLAINED

And when you pray, do not be like the hypocrites, for they love to pray standing in the synagogues and on the street corners to be seen by men. I tell you the truth, they have received their reward in full. But when you pray, go into your room, close the door and pray to your Father, who is unseen. Then your Father, who sees what is done in secret, will reward you. And when you pray, do not keep on babbling like pagans, for they think they will be heard because of their many words. Do not be like them, for your Father knows what you need before you ask him. This, then, is how you should pray:

Our Father in heaven,

hallowed be your name,

your kingdom come,

your will be done

on earth as it is in heaven.

Give us today our daily bread.

Forgive us our debts,

as we also have forgiven our debtors.

And lead us not into temptation,

but deliver us from the evil one.

Matthew 6:5–13 NIV84

The Lord's Prayer was intended as a model for how we should pray, not a prayer that we should repeat every day as our daily prayer. Jesus' intent was just the opposite of that, because the Jews had prayers that they said every day, to be said precisely as they were written and not to be varied. They even had specific prayer times that were not to be violated. It didn't matter where you were or what you were doing, you were commanded to stop and pray. Some Jews made it a point to be in a public place (like on the top steps of the temple) so that everyone would hear them praying and would know how pious they were. Jesus here again was telling people to do just the opposite: They were to pray in private and not to pray repetitive prayers over and over again that eventually lost their effectiveness.

God wants us to pray about what is on our heart and honestly seek Him, because He already knows what we need before we ask Him—but the point is we need to ask. The best way to get yourself in the prayer mode and to feel the moving of the Holy Spirit is to start out your prayer time praising and glorifying the name of God. The Psalms are filled with many praises and prayers that you can read, and they will give you the inspiration for what to pray about.

THE MAKING OF A HERO

> *We know that suffering produces perseverance; perseverance, character; and character, hope.*
>
> Romans 5:3b–4 NIV

Someone asked me recently what makes a hero and who is a hero to me.

A hero isn't necessarily what the world would call a hero. I believe a hero is someone who gets up every day and does his best to serve God and provide for his family in spite of everything that life may throw at him, to try to knock him down.

The first person who comes to my mind is my father, Mack Young. He was a man that definitely fit the description above. He loved God with all of his heart and enjoyed studying the Bible as well as teaching his Sunday school class, which he did for many years. He was someone who would do anything for you and give you the proverbial shirt off his back. He and my mother were polar opposites. While he was outgoing and loved helping people in any way he could, my mother was very reclusive, suffered from severe depression and, probably, bipolar disorder. She was subject to severe mood swings and was very selfish, as well as judgmental. I mention her because my dad, in spite of my mother's problems which he had to deal with almost daily, continued to be very upbeat and never stopped helping people and serving God the best way he could. Everyone loved my dad and always had good things to say about him. I never heard him raise his voice or lose his temper, even to my mother who would go into a violent rage sometimes. My dad would wait until she calmed down and then talk to her about whatever caused her to get so upset. Most of the time I was growing up, he worked two jobs just pay the bills and take care of his family. Even though he needed the money, he would sometimes do handyman jobs for people and not take any money because he knew they couldn't afford to pay him for his services. My dad was a hero to me because he set the example every day of what a man should be and did what he had to do in order to take care of his family, in spite of unpleasant circumstances.

The other person who comes to my mind is James Arness, the actor who played Marshall Matt Dillon on the television series Gunsmoke. As a boy growing up, I idolized Marshall Dillon and wanted to be just like him. Years later, I read about the life of James Arness and discovered he was a hero in real life. During World War II, he was in the Army and stepped on a land mine that almost cost him his leg. He spent a year in a Army hospital in Germany recuperating and learning to walk again. The fact that he was able to perform his own stunts and even get on a horse was a miracle and a testament to his perseverance. Also, James Arness was married to a woman with severe mental and emotional issues and eventually they divorced, leaving him as a single parent with three kids to raise. People criticized him for being very private about his personal life and not granting interviews, but it was because his first priority was his children, and he devoted all his time when not filming Gunsmoke to spending time with them. He was known among his friends as a very generous and caring man who often helped people who were in need. There was a woman who was a hairdresser on the set of Gunsmoke that had cancer, and Jim paid her medical bills for her. Later in her career Amanda Blake, who played Miss Kitty on Gunsmoke, also became very ill, and Jim again paid her medical bills and helped her financially.

Both my father and James Arness knew the meaning of suffering and learned to persevere in spite of what they had to deal with in their lives. That is what being a hero is all about.

Of course, there were many heroes in the Bible. Jesus is the first one to come to mind because he didn't have to do what he did. He suffered severe beatings to the point of being barely conscious, and then was hung on cross, a punishment usually reserved for the worst criminals. It was probably the worst way to die. He went through all of that so you and I could be saved and have the hope of eternal life in heaven with Him.

Greater love has no one than this, than to lay down one's life for his friends.
John 15:13 NKJV

THE MASTER BUILDER

Unless the Lord builds the house, the builders labor in vain. Unless the Lord watches over the city, the guards stand watch in vain.

Psalm 127:1 NIV

If you build a brick house and just stack the bricks on top of one another without using any mortar in between them, the first strong wind will blow the house down.

Just as mortar holds the house together, God is the mortar that holds our lives together. If we put our trust in God, He will watch over us and protect us from the strong winds of life that try to blow us over and destroy us. He is the master builder, and He is the one who gives us the strength and courage to live our lives without fear.

THE POWER OF THE TONGUE

> *The tongue has the power of life and death, and those who love it will eat its fruit.*
>
> Proverbs 18:21 NIV

The tongue is the most powerful muscle in the human body. It has the power to build up and encourage—or to put down and destroy. Its fruit can be very sweet, or extremely bitter. Some people are very good at being encouragers and helping those who need some lifting up. Other people cannot resist being sarcastic and tearing people down, just because they enjoy it or are jealous of that person's success.

We have all said things in a moment of haste or anger that we wish we could take back, but that is why the tongue is so powerful: There is no taking back what we say. Sometimes even an apology is not enough.

Words to live by in a world where it seems everyone has an opinion, and nobody is listening to what is being said. God help us to listen and be obedient to your word. James has a lot to say on this subject:

My dear brothers and sisters, take note of this: Everyone should be quick to listen, slow to speak and slow to become angry.

James 1:19 NIV

THE RETURN OF CHRIST

> *So when the apostles were with Jesus, they kept asking him, "Lord, has the time come for you to free Israel and restore our kingdom?" He replied, "The Father alone has the authority to set those dates and times, and they are not for you to know. But you will receive power when the Holy Spirit comes upon you. And you will be my witnesses, telling people about me everywhere—in Jerusalem, throughout Judea, in Samaria, and to the ends of the earth." After saying this, he was taken up into a cloud while they were watching, and they could no longer see him. As they strained to see him rising into heaven, two white-robed men suddenly stood among them. "Men of Galilee," they said, "why are you standing here staring into heaven? Jesus has been taken from you into heaven, but someday he will return from heaven in the same way you saw him go!"*
>
> Acts 1:6–11 NLT

Jesus will return and appear in the sky. Nobody but God the Father knows exactly when that will happen. Until then, we need to go about our daily lives and live every day as if He is returning today. Being ready is the most important thing we can do. I believe we are living in the last days, but do not believe the false prophets who try to predict the exact date and time Jesus Christ will return. This scripture clearly proves they are liars. As we get closer to Christ's return, the number of false prophets will increase. Believe only what the Bible says. Period.

THE SPIRIT INTERCEDES FOR US

> *In the same way, the Spirit helps us in our weakness. We do not know what we ought to pray for, but the Spirit himself intercedes for us through wordless groans. And he who searches our hearts knows the mind of the Spirit, because the Spirit intercedes for God's people in accordance with the will of God. And we know that in all things God works for the good of those who love him, who have been called according to his purpose.*
>
> Romans 8:26–28 NIV

Have you felt like you should pray about something or someone but didn't know how to pray or what to say? We have all been there; being at a loss for words when you pray is not unusual. That is where the Holy Spirit comes in and prays for us, because He knows our minds and what we want to pray for.

Verse 26 says He "intercedes for us with wordless groans."

For this reason, intercessory prayer is very important. It helps us to pray when we don't know how to pray, especially in very hard situations where life or death is involved. It is hard to know what to say and how to pray for someone's life. Fortunately, God knows our heart and He knows what we are trying to say.

God loves us so much that He knows what we are trying to say before we say it and therefore the Holy Spirit will help us say what we are not able to. What an awesome God we serve—He even knows what we are trying to pray about before we do.

THE WORD WAS GOD

> *In the beginning was the Word, and the Word was with God, and the Word was God. He was in the beginning with God. All things were made through Him, and without Him nothing was made that was made. In Him was life, and the life was the light of men. And the light shines in the darkness, and the darkness did not comprehend it.*
>
> John 1:1–5 NKJV

Jesus Christ is the Word and with his birth He became flesh and blood just like you and me, so that He could be the Living Word, and we could have forgiveness of sin and eternal life through His sacrifice of His life for us.

> *Thomas said to him, "Lord, we don't know where you are going, so how can we know the way?" Jesus answered, "I am the way and the truth and the life. No one comes to the Father except through me. If you really know me, you will know my Father as well. From now on, you do know him and have seen him."*
>
> John 14:5–7 NIV

After His resurrection, the disciples still had a hard time understanding that Jesus is the Christ and the savior they had been looking for. He explained to them that He is the Christ, the Savior, and the Word.

The only way to get to heaven is through Jesus Christ and confessing your sins to Him. There is only one God, and one Savior.

We are indeed thankful that Jesus Christ came to this earth to be born of a virgin, live a normal life, and die on the cross to be our savior; all we have to do is believe He is the Son of God and ask forgiveness of our sins. There is no doubt He is "The way, the truth and the life."

THINGS TO BE THANKFUL FOR

You can be thankful for all the following things that you have received by the grace of God, through Christ Jesus:

- You are beyond condemnation (Romans 8:1);

- You are delivered from the law (Romans 7:6);

- You are near God (Ephesians 2:13);

- You are delivered from the power of evil (Colossians 1:13);

- You are a member of his kingdom (Colossians 1:13);

- You are justified (Romans 5:1);

- You are perfect (Hebrews 10:14);

- You have been adopted (Romans 8:15);

- You have access to God at any moment (Ephesians 2:18);

- You are a part of priesthood (1 Peter 2:5);

- You will never be abandoned (Hebrews 13:5);

- You have an imperishable inheritance (1 Peter 1:4);

- You are a partner with Christ in life (Colossians 3:4), privilege (Ephesians 2:6), suffering (2 Timothy 2:12), and service (1 Corinthians 1:9).

And know that in the heart of God, you are a:

- Member of his body (1 Corinthians 12:13);

- Branch in the vine (John 15:5);

- Stone in the Building (Ephesians 2:19-22);

- Bride for the groom (Ephesians 2:25-27);

- Saint in the new generation (1 Peter 2:9);

- Dwelling place of the spirit (1 Corinthians 6:19).

You possess (Now get this!) every spiritual blessing possible. In Christ, God has given us every spiritual blessing in the heavenly world.

This is the gift offered to the lowliest sinner on earth. Who could make such an offer but God? John 1:16 says, "From him we have all received one gift after another."

TRUST

It is during the darkest times in our lives we have to trust God like we never have before. It is during those times that we become stronger and understand the true depth of God's love and patience with us. Even though we are weak, He is strong and will carry us through the raging storm safely to the other side if we will just hang on and:

> *Trust the lord with all your heart and lean not on your understanding. In all your ways acknowledge him and he will make your paths straight. Do not be wise in your own eyes. Fear the Lord and shun evil. This will bring health to your body and nourishment to your bones.*
>
> Proverbs 3:5–7 NIV84

If you are not trusting in the Lord today, start, and he will become your best friend. There are hundreds of scriptures in the Bible that talk about the love of Christ for those who love Him.

Praise Him today and give Him the Glory.

TRUSTING GOD IN ALL THINGS

> *Trust in the Lord with all your heart,*
> *And lean not on your own understanding;*
> *In all your ways acknowledge Him,*
> *And He shall direct your paths.*
> *Do not be wise in your own eyes;*
> *Fear the Lord and depart from evil.*
> *It will be health to your flesh,*
> *And strength to your bones*
> *Proverbs 3:5–8 NKJV*

There are times when we really need to pray and trust God more than ever. Leaning on our own understanding like the scripture above says is never the right thing to do. We should always trust God because He knows what is the right thing to do and what is going to happen in the future. God is the only one we can trust all the time. Putting our faith and trust in others is very risky because they are human just like us and they mean well, but they could lead you in the wrong direction. Just because something seems right, that doesn't necessarily mean that it is.

TRUTH

We are living this prophecy by the Apostle Paul right now.

People are not looking for the truth, but someone who will tell them what they want to hear. History is no longer taught in schools, and pastors are afraid of preaching the truth for fear of offending someone and losing parishioners. Politicians tell people what they want to hear just to get votes. The truth is—and always will be—what really matters, because no matter how hard you try, you cannot change it. Don't just assume someone is telling the truth, check it out for yourself. Too many people today are not telling the truth just to have their way.

> *Jesus said to him, "I am the way, the truth, and the life. No one comes to the Father except through Me."*
>
> John 14:6 NKJV

When Jesus was walking this earth, people were lying and cheating to keep him from telling the truth. For political reasons, they wanted to have things their way and they could not understand that Jesus wasn't interested in politics, but people's souls. Things really haven't changed much in the last 2000 years: politicians today are lying because they want to stay in power or attain power. If you put your trust in Jesus and His word, the Bible says you won't have to worry about the truth, because He is the truth.

UNCONDITIONAL FAITH

> *The Lord had said to Abram, "Leave your country, your people and your father's household and go to the land I will show you. I will make you into a great nation and I will bless you; I will make your name great, and you will be a blessing. I will bless those who bless you, and whoever curses you I will curse; and all peoples on earth will be blessed through you."*
>
> Genesis 12:1–10 NIV84

Abraham was seventy-five years old. He had lived in Haran a very long time and was very prosperous and contented. God told him to pack up everything he had and go to a place that He would show him. Can you imagine being seventy-five years old and God comes to you, telling you to move away from the place you had lived most of your life, and you don't know where?

You are just to pack up your family and everything you own and let God tell you where to go. Remember, Abraham was a very rich man and had a lot of land and livestock; a lifetime of work went into what he had. Surely Abraham had a lot of faith in God and trusted Him completely.

I think most people would balk at doing such a thing. They would say something like, "Come on God, I am seventy-five years old, and I have this place just the way I want it. I am ready to retire right here."

"Why are you asking me to do something this huge, moving everything I own and my family someplace, I don't even know where?" But he didn't; he trusted God completely and traveled a long way to get to where God wanted him to be. This wasn't traveling in an RV or comfortable vehicle; this was walking every mile of the way.

Would you have that kind of faith, to do what God is telling and not question him?

Just be obedient and know that God knows what is best for you. As it turned out, Abraham was richly blessed with more than he had in Haran. Most people have trouble trusting God for small things. Abraham was the father of the Jewish people and was highly respected for his absolute faith in God. His example of trusting God completely is one of the most inspiring stories in the Bible. I would say most of us would have trouble having that kind of faith.

UNITY IN CHRIST

> *There is one body and one Spirit, just as you were called in one hope of your calling; one Lord, one faith, one baptism; one God and Father of all, who is above all, and through all, and in you all.*
>
> Ephesians 4:4–6 NKJV

Following Christ and being unified under Him as one body was the original idea that Christ instructed us to do before he ascended back into heaven. Religion and denominations were not what Jesus Christ and the apostles had in mind. Just as in everything else, men could not agree on what to do and Satan caused them to become divided. As a result, many different churches and denominations popped up over a period of several hundred years, beginning with the Roman Catholic Church and their attempt to rule the church. Martin Luther was largely responsible for people breaking away from the Catholic Church. Today there are many different churches and denominations.

When people ask me what to look for in a church, I always tell them to look for several common denominators that unify most Protestant churches. These churches:

- Believe Jesus was born of a virgin,

- Believe he was crucified on the cross,

- Believe he was resurrected on the third day,

- Believe he is now seated beside God on the throne of heaven,

- Believe in the plan of salvation; that Jesus Christ died on the cross for your sins and you must ask Him for forgiveness of your sins in order to be saved and call Him your Lord and Savior.

There are many other traditions that churches do in many different ways, if they do them at all: Baptism, communion, speaking in tongues, offerings, and church government.

The five main elements I listed are the most important things to look for. The other things are a matter of what you are comfortable with.

Be very much in prayer and ask God to guide you, through His Holy Spirit, to the church that is right for you. It is not a matter of right or wrong, but a matter of preference.

WAITING ON THE LORD TO RETURN

> Dear friends, here is one thing you must not forget. With the Lord a day is like a thousand years. And a thousand years are like a day. The Lord is not slow to keep his promise. He is not slow in the way some people understand it. Instead, he is patient with you. He doesn't want anyone to be destroyed. Instead, he wants all people to turn away from their sins. But the day of the Lord will come like a thief. The heavens will disappear with a roar. Fire will destroy everything in them. God will judge the earth and everything done in it.
>
> So everything will be destroyed in this way. And what kind of people should you be? You should lead holy and godly lives. Live like this as you look forward to the day of God. Living like this will make the day come more quickly. On that day fire will destroy the heavens. Its heat will melt everything in them. But we are looking forward to a new heaven and a new earth. Godliness will live there. All this is in keeping with God's promise.
>
> Dear friends, I know you are looking forward to this. So try your best to be found pure and without blame. Be at peace with God. Remember that while our Lord is waiting patiently to return, people are being saved.
>
> 2 Peter 3:8–15 NIrV

Peter is telling people not to be impatient; the Lord always keeps his promises. He promised he would return, and He will, but it will be in His timing. A day is like a thousand years to the Lord, and we are to go about our daily lives as we normally do. We are not to be sitting around waiting on His return, but to be prepared because He could come anytime. One of the reasons He hasn't returned is He wants as many people to be saved as possible and nobody left behind. He will return when the time is right, and people are no longer responding to His word. We are living in a time when church attendance has declined sharply over the last several years, and people are doing whatever they feel like doing and being drawn to worldly pleasures.

There are things happening today that I never thought would be done in my lifetime. People have no shame.

As Christians we have to do our best to live our lives for Christ. We need to tell others about Christ and how they can be saved. While we are looking forward to a glorious new heaven and earth, we should also want no one to be lost. The Lord is patient, but his patience won't last forever.

WEALTHY BUT POOR

Now listen, you rich people, weep and wail because of the misery that is coming upon you. Your wealth has rotted, and moths have eaten your clothes. Your gold and silver are corroded. Their corrosion will testify against you and eat your flesh like fire. You have hoarded wealth in the last days. Look! The wages you failed to pay the workmen who mowed your fields are crying out against you. The cries of the harvesters have reached the ears of the Lord Almighty. You have lived on earth in luxury and self-indulgence. You have fattened yourselves in the day of slaughter. You have condemned and murdered innocent men, who were not opposing you.

James 5:1–6 NIV 84

What is going in today's economy, with people abusing their wealth at the expense of everyone else, is really nothing new. The Bible has a lot to say about those who abuse their wealth and what will happen to them in the end. James talks about two things in this passage: First, about the ultimate worthlessness of earthly riches and second, about the questionable character of some who possess wealth. He is trying to tell people: Don't put all your hopes in earthly things because it is all going to be gone some day. Rich people who abuse their wealth will face severe punishment and be judged accordingly. He says the rich will weep and wail at the misery they will face on judgment day. The word he uses for wail means to shriek or to howl in an unbearable agony that will not cease. The insatiable desire for wealth and earthly possessions is like a terrible rust that eats into people's souls and their bodies. It becomes a consuming fire that eventually destroys them. That is exactly what is happening today: People are being destroyed by their own selfishness and greed, thinking only of themselves and not those who have invested in their banks and worked hard to earn what they have. The people who cannot afford to lose money are the ones being hurt most by what is happening on Wall Street today. This passage also talks about how people treat their employees by cheating them out of their wages and not paying them what they deserve.

James is saying that there are selfish rich people who have gained their wealth by cheating others and cheating their employees. He is saying they have used their wealth for their own self gratification and worldly pleasures. The Greek word translated to live in soft luxury is *truphao*. It comes from a root word which means to break down and describes the kind of soft living which destroys a person's moral strength. The word which is translated luxury is *spatalao*. It is a much harsher description which means to live shameless lives of excess, to satisfy your own lusts at the expense of others. Anyone who chooses to use their wealth to satisfy their own greed is on a path to eternal condemnation.

WHAT GOD IS THINKING

> For My thoughts are not your thoughts,
> Nor are your ways My ways," says the Lord.
> "For as the heavens are higher than the earth,
> So are My ways higher than your ways,
> And My thoughts than your thoughts.
>
> Isaiah 55:8 NIV

Have you ever thought to yourself, "What was God thinking?! Why did He let this happen? Why did He take my loved one?" Sometimes, it is very hard to accept what happens in our lives. We even get mad at God because our prayers aren't answered. God sees things that we don't; He knows what is best and what the future holds. We cannot even fathom God's ways—and we could not handle it if we could.

God loves us so much that He protects us from things we don't even know are happening. Our job is to trust God and to believe that He hears and answers our prayers, maybe not in the way we want, but in the way that is best.

WHAT THE LORD REQUIRES

> *No, O people, the Lord has told you what is good,*
> *and this is what he requires of you:*
> *to do what is right, to love mercy,*
> *and to walk humbly with your God.*
>
> Micah 6:8 NLT

I have had people tell me that being a Christian is too hard and it is too late for them after everything they have done.

It is never too late to let Jesus Christ into your life, and Christ can make your life easier if you are willing to let him. The prophet Micah tells us that the Lord wants us to do right. I think everyone wants to do the right thing, even though it may be difficult. Christ can help you make the right choices in your life, ones that will make your life easier.

We are to love mercy. We all want mercy and giving mercy to others is something that not only is the right thing to do, but it makes us feel good when we help someone that is in need of mercy and help. We are to walk humbly with our God. Being humble is probably the hardest thing for us to do, because pride gets in the way. Nobody likes to admit they are wrong or do what Christ is asking us to do. Sometimes, He is telling us to do something that in our minds doesn't make sense. I have had to make decisions in my life that at the time did not make sense and do what the Lord was asking me to do. Later on, looking back, I understood why the Lord had me do it, and I was glad that I listened to Him because it was the best thing for me at that time. What the Lord requires is for us to listen to the voice of His Holy Spirit and be obedient to Him; and that is a lot easier than you might think because His way is always the right way

WHAT'S IN IT FOR ME?

Then James and John, the sons of Zebedee, came to him. "Teacher," they said, "we want you to do for us whatever we ask."

"What do you want me to do for you?" he asked.

They replied, "Let one of us sit at your right and the other at your left in your glory."

"You don't know what you are asking," Jesus said. "Can you drink the cup I drink or be baptized with the baptism I am baptized with?"

"We can," they answered.

Jesus said to them, "You will drink the cup I drink and be baptized with the baptism I am baptized with, but to sit at my right or left is not for me to grant. These places belong to those for whom they have been prepared."

When the ten heard about this, they became indignant with James and John. Jesus called them together and said, "You know that those who are regarded as rulers of the Gentiles lord it over them, and their high officials exercise authority over them. Not so with you. Instead, whoever wants to become great among you must be your servant, and whoever wants to be first must be slave of all. For even the Son of Man did not come to be served, but to serve, and to give his life as a ransom for many."

Mark 10:35–45 NIV

Jesus didn't call us to greatness, He called us to service. He didn't call us to lord our Christianity over those who are less fortunate than we are. He called us do what we can to help those around us, who need extra help in order to be able to live. Some people think that in order to be a Christian you have to be a middle-class white person. There are people that, if someone walks into their church and isn't dressed as nice as they are, they look down at them and ignore them instead of treating them like a child of God who needs His love and the compassion of those in the church. Somewhere Christians have gotten the idea that being a Christian is supposed to be cozy and comfortable and we are to insulate ourselves from those who aren't just like us.

The disciples had gotten the mistaken idea that the Kingdom of Heaven was going to be like earthly kingdoms, and they would be rewarded in heaven by sitting on a throne beside Jesus. Jesus tried to explain to them what he was going to have go through in order go back to heaven and asked them if they could do those things. They did not understand and would not understand until Christ was crucified on the cross. Then they realized, in order to serve Jesus Christ, they were going to have to risk their lives and eventually die proclaiming Him as their savior.

Keep on loving each other as brothers. Do not forget to entertain strangers,
for by so doing some people have entertained angels without knowing it.
Hebrews 13:1–2 NIV84

We never know, when talking to someone, if there is going to be an opportunity to share the love of Christ with them, and possibly change their life. Sometimes a kind word from a stranger will make that person's day. Sometimes we get so preoccupied with what is going on in our own lives that we fail to notice the needs of those around us. Being a Christian isn't just going to church on Sunday morning and warming a chair; being a Christian is showing the love of Jesus in our everyday lives.

Many people don't go to church today because they feel out of place and not worthy of being there. Jesus' mission on earth was to make everyone welcome in the Kingdom of Heaven. He didn't speak in the synagogues, nor did he stay with Jewish leaders of the time. Jesus went out among the people. It didn't matter if they were poor or didn't wear nice clothes, He cared about their souls and He slept wherever he could. He was homeless and—if He were on Earth today—He would be hanging out in homeless shelters and with street people. How big the church you attend doesn't matter—how big your heart is for finding lost souls and leading them to the Savior is what matters.

The one and only mission of the church, all churches, is to lead people Christ, nothing else matters.

WHEN THOUGHTS BECOME SIN

"I am not referring to all of you; I know those I have chosen. But this is to fulfill the scripture: 'He who shares my bread has lifted up his heel against me.' I am telling you now before it happens, so that when it does happen you will believe that I am He. I tell you the truth, whoever accepts anyone I send accepts me; and whoever accepts me accepts the one who sent me."

After he had said this, Jesus was troubled in spirit and testified, "I tell you the truth, one of you is going to betray me."

His disciples stared at one another, at a loss to know which of them he meant. One of them, the disciple whom Jesus loved, was reclining next to him. Simon Peter motioned to this disciple and said, "Ask him which one he means."

Leaning back against Jesus, he asked him, "Lord, who is it?"

Jesus answered, "It is the one to whom I will give this piece of bread when I have dipped it in the dish." Then, dipping the piece of bread, he gave it to Judas Iscariot, son of Simon. As soon as Judas took the bread, Satan entered into him.

"What you are about to do, do quickly," Jesus told him.

John 13:18–27 NIV

In John, Chapter 13, Jesus talks about how one of his disciples will betray him. Have you ever wondered how Judas could do such a thing to Jesus as to betray him and turn him over to the Pharisees? How could someone follow Jesus around for three years, listen to his teaching, watch all the miracles He performed, and betray Him? John said that Satan entered into him as soon as he took the bread from Jesus. That tells us that Judas had free will and up to that point he could have backed out of his plan and not betrayed Jesus. Up to that point, Judas had not sinned, but by accepting the bread he formed the intent to carry out his plan to betray Jesus. Our thoughts don't become sin until we act on them; just thinking about something isn't sin. But when we actually form the intention to carry out what we have been thinking, then it becomes sin. It could be that Judas had thought about betraying Jesus, but he never actually thought about how he was going to do it until that night in the upper room.

Judas didn't realize the serious consequences of his actions until he had already betrayed Jesus and found out they were going to kill Him. He just thought they would put Him in prison, maybe whip Him and let Him go. He didn't realize Jesus was going to die, even though Jesus had predicted his death. In Judas' defense, none of the other disciples believed Him when He said He was going to die. That's the thing about sin; we really have no idea how far reaching the consequences of our actions are going to be until it is too late, and we can't undo what we have done. If someone goes out and has an affair, they don't realize how far reaching the consequences of their actions are going to be and how many people it is going to hurt. They are so consumed with lust and the passion of the moment they are blinded to the consequences. The same thing with telling a lie. It seems so innocent when you tell it, but pretty soon you have to tell another one to cover the original lie, and before you know it the truth becomes a blur, and you can't take back what you already said. Judas, after he realized Jesus was going to be killed, gave the money back he had been given to betray Jesus, hoping he could somehow relieve his guilt, but it didn't work. It was too late, and he couldn't stop what was happening. In despair he went out and hanged himself. Jesus' death and resurrection had been predicted thousands of years before (see Isaiah 53). Judas was the instrument Satan used to carry out his plan for Jesus' death.

There are so many people today that get so deep in sin, that they think there is no way out of their situation. They commit suicide and don't realize that Jesus died so that they could have forgiveness of those sins. Suicide is never the answer. Satan wants people to think there is no way out, but it is not true. There is nothing that anyone has ever done that cannot be forgiven by the blood of Jesus. Jesus said let him who has not sinned cast the first stone.

Sin is such a subtle thing, and it can enter into our lives and our hearts before we even realize what we are doing.

If you are carrying around a load of guilt and want to get rid of it, all you have to do is ask Jesus to forgive you and He will forgive you and forget it ever happened.

WHY GOD LOVES YOU

> *For God so loved the world that he gave his one and only Son, that whoever believes in him shall not perish but have eternal life. For God did not send his Son into the world to condemn the world, but to save the world through him. Whoever believes in him is not condemned, but whoever does not believe stands condemned already because they have not believed in the name of God's one and only Son.*
>
> John 3:16–18 NIV84

Jesus was born for one reason and that was to die on the cross for our sins. As we celebrate His birth this month, we should also remember He was born to be the sacrificial lamb for our sins.

Can you imagine knowing you were going to be born into this world just so you could die and be the human sacrificial lamb for all the sin in the world? Not only that, but to die on the cross, one of the most horrible and agonizing ways to die. That would take a lot of courage; to live a life knowing what you were facing.

Be thankful that God sent His son into the world to be born and to die, that we may have forgiveness of our sins and the hope of eternal life with our Lord and Savior Jesus Christ. As we celebrate the birth of our Savior, thank Him for everything His birth represents in each of our lives. Thank Him and give Him all the praise and the glory every day of the year.

WHY HAVEN'T I BEEN HEALED?

> *And I will do whatever you ask in my name, so that the Father may be glorified in the Son. You may ask me for anything in my name, and I will do it.*
>
> John 14:13–14 NIV

"Why haven't I been healed?" That's a question a lot of people who are suffering ask, and one that has confounded people for thousands of years. We look at things from our human perspective and how much pain we are in, but God looks at it from His perspective and whether it will glorify Him. Everything God does is intended to bring glory to Him and His name. I have known many very Godly people who asked God for healing and were not healed, and others who were miraculously healed—including myself. The thing is, all things have to be according to the will of God and not our individual desires. The apostle Paul asked God to remove what he called the thorn in his side three times and was not healed, yet God used Paul mightily in spite of whatever physical issue he had. God can use you in spite of your physical limitations. Don't wait for your healing to ask God to use you. It just could be what God is waiting on; for you to say, "Yes, Lord, I am willing to be used however and wherever you want me, and I won't let my physical limitations become a crutch for me not to be used for your glory."

Healing is a glorious and wonderful thing as long as you give God all the glory.

There are people today who have not been healed and God is using them in glorious ways to bring people to Christ. One such person is Joni Eareckson Tada. Joni really puts things in perspective with this quote:

One problem I have with faith-healing is that it tends to be focused only on the physical aspect of healing. But Jesus always backed away when people came to him only to get their physical needs met. My goodness, he was ready to have you lop off your hand! His real interest was in healing the soul.[1]

In other words, Jesus wants you to be healed spiritually more than physically.

All I can say to that is AMEN! What good would it do for someone to be healed physically and not spiritually? It would be very sad for someone to be physically healed and go to hell.

---

1. "Why Does God Allow Suffering?" *Time,* September 8th, 2010

WISDOM

> *Oh, the depth of the riches of the wisdom and knowledge of God!*
>
> *How unsearchable his judgments,*
>
> *and his paths beyond tracing out!*
>
> *Who has known the mind of the Lord?*
>
> *Or who has been his counselor?*
>
> *Who has ever given to God*
>
> *that God should repay him?*
>
> *For from him and through him and to him are all things.*
>
> *To him be the glory forever! Amen.*
>
> Romans 11:33–36 NIV

How can we even begin to compare ourselves to God? God's wisdom and judgments are so far above ours that we cannot even fathom what God is thinking. All we have to do is look around us to see the glory of God. God spoke the universe into existence. When was the last time you spoke and, voila, there it was, your fondest dream come true, just through your word? There is an old song that says in part, "When you wish upon a star, makes no difference who you are, anything your heart desires will come to you." Wishing upon a star doesn't accomplish anything, other than wishful thinking—and a stiff neck.

But if we put the desires of our heart in the hands of the one who created the universe, our needs will be taken care of. Verse 36 says, "For from him and through him and to him are all things." God doesn't' need our advice; He is not looking for us to advise Him on how He should bless us and meet our needs. God needs our obedience, and through our obedience, He will give us the wisdom to make the right choices in our lives, choices that will bring honor and glory to Him. All of this is absolutely free, Jesus already paid for it on the cross. People pay thousands of dollars to mental health professionals and so called life coaches to find out how to get the most out of life. God tells us that if we only look to Him, we don't have to look any further. Whose advice would you rather have, the God of the universe or another human being?

YES AND NO

> *Again, you have heard that it was said to the people long ago, "Do not break your oath, but keep the oaths you have made to the Lord." But I tell you, do not swear at all: either by heaven, for it is God's throne; or by the earth, for it is his footstool; or by Jerusalem, for it is the city of the Great King. And do not swear by your head, for you cannot make even one hair white or black. Simply let your 'Yes' be 'Yes,' and your 'No,' 'No'; anything beyond this comes from the evil one.*
>
> Matthew 5:33–37 NIV84

In this portion of scripture, Jesus is saying don't make a promise that you are going to do something. Your word should be enough for you to follow through with what you say you will do. If you say no to something, then mean no and do not waver on your decision. Oaths were a very serious thing in biblical times. If you made an oath or a promise to do something, your word was expected to be kept. If you didn't fulfill that oath there could be very serious consequences. In the days before written contracts, an oral contract was considered just as binding. Even today, the Quakers still consider their word to be a binding contract and they refuse to take an oath or swear to anything, because they always tell the truth and there is no reason to take an oath promising to tell the truth because they already do that. The reason today why people have to swear to tell the truth in court is because people lie, even under oath, on the Bible, before God. We have written contracts that are very complicated and that no one but a lawyer can understand because people are deceitful and will find any reason they can to get out of a contract.

I read a story about a preacher who was going to preach on honesty the next Sunday and he told the congregation to read Joshua Chapter 25 that coming week. The next Sunday he asked, "How many of you read Joshua Chapter 25 this week?" About half of the people raised their hands. "Now you are the people I want to talk to. The book of Joshua has only 24 chapters, so I am especially concerned about you."

YOU ARE MINE

But now, thus says the Lord, who created you, O Jacob,

And He who formed you, O Israel:

"Fear not for I have redeemed you;

I have called you by your name;

You are Mine.

When you pass through the waters,

I will be with you;

And through the rivers, they shall not overflow you.

When you walk through the fire, you shall not be burned,

Nor shall the flame scorch you.

For I am the Lord your God,

The Holy One of Israel, your Savior;

Isaiah 43:1–3 NKJV

It is important to remember that no matter what happens in life, the Lord will be with you and keep you from harm. It is very easy to have fear and doubt, but fear not—the Lord God will be with you. Did you know that the words "fear not" are in the Bible 365 times! I think the Lord is trying to tell us something! Every generation since the time of

Christ has had different things to be afraid of, and the Lord has been there throughout each generation. There have been wars and rumors of wars for thousands of years, even before the birth of Christ. The only reliable source of peace is our Lord and Savior Jesus Christ. He gives us the victory every time.

YOU CAN'T LIE TO GOD

> *All the believers were one in heart and mind. No one claimed that any of his posses-sions was his own, but they shared everything they had. With great power the apostles continued to testify to the resurrection of the Lord Jesus, and much grace was upon them all. There were no needy persons among them. For from time to time those who owned lands or houses sold them, brought the money from the sales and put it at the apostles' feet, and it was distributed to anyone as he had need. Joseph, a Levite from Cyprus, whom the apostles called Barnabas (which means Son of Encour-agement), sold a field he owned and brought the money and put it at the apostles' feet.*
>
> Acts 4:32–36 NIV84

People were excited at what was happening; they were witnessing the power of the Holy Spirit. The people were all filled with the power of the Holy Spirit and there was a sense of unity among them to the point they pooled all of their possessions and helped each other with their needs. People even sold houses and land and gave the money to Peter and John to use it as they saw fit. Barnabas is thought to be the rich young ruler who approached Jesus earlier about what he had to do to be saved.

Unfortunately though, not everyone has pure motives when it comes to doing things in the name of God or in the name of the church:

> *Now a man named Ananias, together with his wife Sapphira, also sold a piece of property. With his wife's full knowledge he kept back part of the money for himself, but brought the rest and put it at the apostles' feet. Then Peter said, "Ananias, how is it that Satan has so filled your heart that you have lied to the Holy Spirit and have kept for yourself some of the money you received for the land? Didn't it belong to you before it was sold? And after it was sold, wasn't the money at your disposal? What made you think of doing such a thing? You have not lied to men but to God."*
>
> *When Ananias heard this, he fell down and died. And great fear seized all who heard what had happened. Then the young men came forward, wrapped up his body, and carried him out and buried him.*
>
> *About three hours later his wife came in, not knowing what had happened. Peter asked her, "Tell me, is this the price you and Ananias got for the land?"*
>
> *"Yes," she said, "that is the price."*
>
> *Peter said to her, "How could you agree to test the Spirit of the Lord? Look! The feet of the men who buried your husband are at the door, and they will carry you out also."*
>
> *At that moment she fell down at his feet and died. Then the young men came in and, finding her dead, carried her out and buried her beside her husband. Great fear seized the whole church and all who heard about these events.*
>
> Acts 5:1–12 NIV84

There was no reason at all for Ananias to lie and try to make himself look as if he were extremely generous by saying he had sold this land and given all of the money to the apostles. All of the people who were giving things were doing it voluntarily, no one pressuring anybody to give beyond what they felt God was telling them to give. All Ananias had to do was be honest about his plans for the money. It wasn't the fact that he had kept some money for himself—it was that he lied about it. He was trying to make himself look good in front of other people, while being greedy and deceitful at the same time. He saw what Barnabas and others had done and wanted to look good in front of the others.

He was trying to have it both ways. You can't serve God and lie to God at the same time. Peter told him he wasn't lying to men but lying to God. There is no evidence that Peter knew about this in advance; it was through the Holy Spirit he was told about the sin and deceitfulness of Ananias and Sapphira. You may be able to lie to people, but God knows your heart:

> *The heart is deceitful above all things*
> *and beyond cure.*
> *Who can understand it?*
> *"I the Lord search the heart*
> *and examine the mind,*
> *to reward a man according to his conduct,*
> *according to what his deeds deserve."*
>
> Jeremiah 17:9–11 NIV84

ABOUT THE AUTHOR

Jim Young served 23 years in the Army and after retiring, he became an ordained minister. He has been a pastor and a hospice chaplain. Jim and his wife Kathy live in Show Low, Arizona. They have 3 children, 7 grandchildren, and 1 great-grandchild.

Milton Keynes UK
Ingram Content Group UK Ltd.
UKHW012316150324
439374UK00015B/865